Foreword

Getting off to a good start

For the enthusiastic entrepreneur, the setting up of that first company is a unique event. As bankers, we can share our customers' excitement and at the same time contribute the know-how we have acquired from our involvement with other customers.

Our experience has been built up over the centuries and augmented, we believe, by regular inputs of ingenuity, from the day in August 1728 when we allowed Mr William Hogg, a merchant in the High Street, Edinburgh, to take out of the bank more than he had put in – and thereby invented the overdraft – to our latest in electronic desk-top banking.

The first in a series of books is designed specifically for new businesses, to help simplify the launch and guarantee a healthy organization with a long, happy and profitable lifespan.

Bob Maiden
Managing Director
The Royal Bank of Scotland

The Royal Bank of Scotland

Starting a Small Business

Nigel Hill

Letts

First published 1990
by Charles Letts & Co Ltd
Diary House, Borough Road, London SE1 1DW

British Library Cataloguing in Publication Data
Hill, Nigel
    Starting a small business
    1. Great Britain. Small firms. Organization
    I. Title II. Royal Bank of Scotland III. Series
    658'.022'0941

ISBN 0–85097–880–7

The Author

Nigel Hill BSc(Econ), MPhil, DipM, MCIM is Marketing Director of JPD
Associates Ltd, a company with interests in management consultancy, training and
manufacturing. He has published numerous articles and two textbooks on
marketing, and is author of the companion volume *Successful Marketing for Small
Businesses*. Nigel has previously worked in management positions in the
manufacturing, retailing and service sectors, largely with small companies. In his
current role he provides marketing, business planning and training support to
JPD's clients. He has assisted in the starting up of many small firms and businesses.

Readers please note: Some of the information in this book, particularly that which is directly
influenced by government policy, and the contact addresses and telephone numbers of useful
organizations, is liable to change. From May 1990 the London telephone code *01* will be
replaced by *071* or *081*.
    It should also be noted that, where words have been used which denote the masculine
gender only, they shall be deemed to include the feminine gender, and vice versa.

Printed and bound in Great Britain by
Charles Letts (Scotland) Ltd

Contents

Setting Up in Business

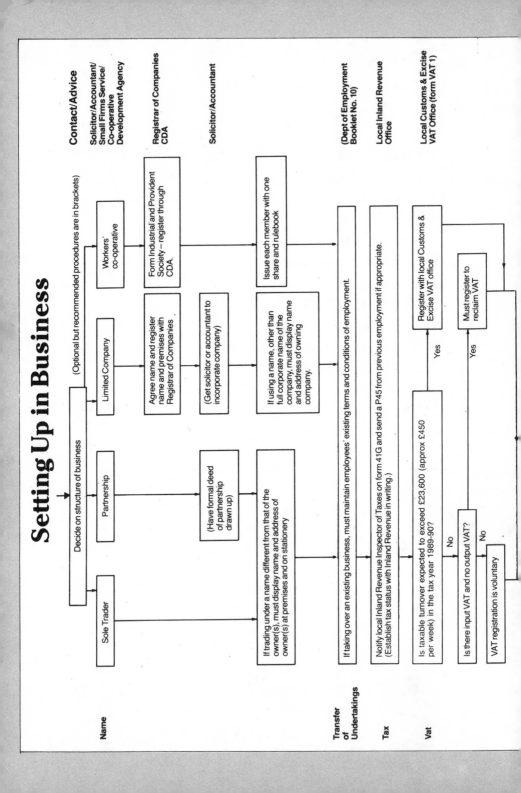

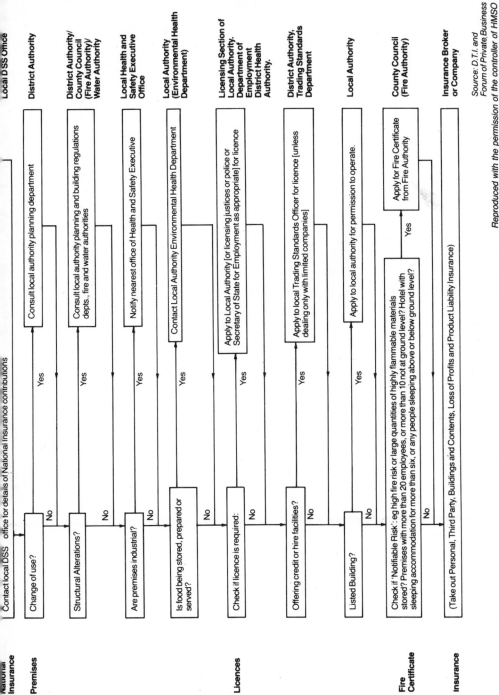

Source: D.T.I. and Forum of Private Business

Reproduced with the permission of the controller of HMSO

1 Personal demands

Aims of this chapter

This chapter will examine the pros and cons of starting your own business in order to help you to decide whether or not it is the right decision for you as an individual. It will look at:

- Personal characteristics of successful businessmen
- People's motives for starting their own business
- The importance of family circumstances
- Business skills and knowledge required

Readers wishing to explore this topic in greater detail are recommended to consult:

New Enterprises: A Start-up Case Book, S. Birley, Croom Helm, 1982.

Small Businesses and Entrepreneurship, eds. P. Burns and J. Dewhurst, Macmillan, 1989.

The aptitudes of aspiring male and female entrepreneurs, S. Cromie in *Small Business Development: Some Current Issues*, eds. O'Neill, Bhambri, Faulkner and Cannon, Avebury/Gower, 1987.

The successful type

Much has been written over the years about the characteristics of successful businessmen in the hope of discovering what they have in common, presumably so that these magic ingredients can be reproduced. However, there is no secret formula. In practice, successful businessmen come from a variety of backgrounds, but research has shown that many of them do share certain general characteristics and attitudes. These may have helped them to succeed, so let's have a closer look at them. Most studies show that five general characteristics are shared by the large majority of successful businessmen, particularly the ones who start out with nothing and build up thriving businesses. These characteristics will now be briefly dealt with.

What are successful businessmen like?

1 **They are hard workers.** If you're going to start a small business from scratch and make it grow into a reasonable size, you'll have to be prepared to work very hard. Successful

entrepreneurs are often people who continue to work for fourteen hours a day even when they're multi-millionaires, because they **like** doing it. They obviously don't need the money any more. Quite simply, their work, and being successful at it, is more important to them than almost anything else in life.

2 They are achievers. Whether running a business, running a race, playing squash or even playing *Trivial Pursuit*, successful businessmen are achievers. They want to win, and they try very, very hard to be winners at all things. In business they particularly want to be more successful than their competitors. They set themselves goals and are prepared to make any sacrifice necessary to reach them. Family, friends, socializing, recreation – all will often take second place.

3 They are controllers. Successful businessmen like being in control of their own future. This means making decisions, using initiative, taking the first step, and taking risks if necessary. Many people would find this stressful, but good businessmen will not make a decision and then worry about whether they made the right one. They are much too busy making the next decision and the one after that. Compared to most people they suffer less from stress and worry despite leading a more 'stressful' life. Above all they never sit back and wait for things to happen. They always make sure that they are actively involved in **making** them happen.

4 They are firm and decisive. Good businessmen know that they cannot afford to be 'soft'. They will not tolerate failure in themselves or in anyone else. They will act quickly and without sentiment to rid themselves of a person, a product or a project if it becomes clear that it is not successful.

5 They hate wasting time. Successful businessmen respect time and never waste it. They make sure that every minute is used fully. This applies to their free time as well. They are always punctual and expect others to be the same.

This attitude towards time is very important in explaining their success. Many people, at work and in their private lives, manage to waste a tremendous amount of their time, and productive work often amounts to a horrifyingly small proportion of time. Much of the day can be spent in all sorts of unproductive ways:

a getting from A to B
b day dreaming
c having casual conversations
d watching television
e eating
f 'faffing about'

'Faffing about' is the worst offender of all. It involves being extremely busy doing something utterly trivial, and successful businessmen don't do it!

Are you the right type?

Do you have these five characteristics? It does not mean to say that you can't be successful if you don't have them all, but a person who possesses a good proportion of all these attributes is certainly likely to work in a single-minded way towards the achievement of his objectives. By his very nature, making a success of his business will be more important to him than anything else.

However, many would argue that it's better to keep things a little more in proportion. Most people with a business have other priorities as well as running their business successfully: having a happy marriage and bringing up their children well, for example. It is not the purpose of this book to tell people what their priorities should be but to outline good techniques for starting a successful business, and there is no doubt that being single-minded will help you to do this. The best policy if you have a family is to nominate certain times of the day and week as 'family times' and enjoy them to the full. Then, during the 'business times' you can aim to be 100 per cent single minded, efficient, decisive and very hard working. At least you can aim to be!

Motives

Before reading the rest of this section, write down the three main reasons why you want to start your own business. It is generally accepted that some reasons for starting a business are more appropriate than others.

The 'right' reasons

1 **Ambition.** An ambitious person who likes to succeed in everything he does will often start a business with a certain target in mind, for example, to reach a £1 million turnover within five years, or to open three shops within three years. Provided you are prepared for all the hard work that is necessary to achieve your aim, this kind of ambition can often be the ideal ingredient to fuel success.

2 **Responsibility and independence.** Strong-minded people who are looking for the opportunity to make decisions and control the destiny of an organization are often well suited to the task of running a business. You may feel that you could do a better job of running your present organization, department or company than some of your superiors. If you do feel that you need some real

responsibility, running your own business could provide the ideal challenge.

3 Ideas. Having a good idea can be an excellent reason for wanting to start a business but nobody can be absolutely certain that a good idea will develop into a commercial success. Many apparently brilliant ideas developed by very clever people and by very large companies actually turn out to be flops in the market place. One of the attributes of successful businessmen is said to be their ability to pick the one commercial winner from a whole bag full of good ideas. But nobody has a perfect track record of recognizing the good ideas from the bad ones. A well-known company rejected a 'good idea' for a domestic work bench because they felt it would never catch on. Correctly identified as a winner by another company, that product is now known as the Black and Decker *Workmate*! Chapter 2 will look more closely at the methods of evaluating the potential of business ideas.

The 'wrong' reasons

1 A way of escape from your present job. Disliking your job is certainly one reason for taking action and seeking an alternative but it is not a good enough reason in itself for considering self-employment as the right alternative. It cannot be stressed too strongly that self-employment is not an easy option, so it is vital to have a number of positive reasons for wanting to run your own business.

2 Making lots of money. Is this a good enough reason for wanting to start your own business? Will going it alone enable you to make your fortune?

If you have a job with a salary close to or above the national average you may well end up no better off financially if you set up your own business, and you will be taking far greater risks to maintain your standard of living. You will almost certainly have to work much harder, too.

Having said that, if your ambition is to make yourself a millionaire, there is no doubt that the best way to achieve this is to start your own business. Many people still start businesses with nothing and succeed in making themselves very rich, but they are in the minority.

Family circumstances

Are your family circumstances appropriate for starting a business?

This is a vital question to consider at this stage because starting a business will almost certainly have profound consequences for your family life. On the one hand, it can be very exciting and unite everyone in your family. In their early days, many small businesses have been kept going by family members lending a willing hand. Running a business can bring families together, providing goals and daily tasks which are shared by all its members. In fact, so important is the support of the family that it is reckoned that one of the main reasons for small business failures is lack of family support. It is important to be aware of the main difficulties that can arise for your family when you start your own business.

Lack of time

Involving the family in the business as much as is practical is a very good idea. They will then associate with it more easily and will find it easier to accept the difficulties that you are placing upon them. The family must understand and accept that the business will demand long hours and hard work from you. This means that you may not be able to spend as much time with them as you would like. You may have to suddenly cancel days or evenings out which the family had been looking forward to for some time. You will always seem to be dashing in and dashing out again. This is bound to make the family feel neglected, but if you have discussed the problem with them in advance they are more likely to cope when the time comes. They must understand how important it is for you to succeed and will need to be convinced that their sacrifice is necessary for the business to be successful.

Lack of money

Until the business is well established your family may have to face a fall in their standard of living. New businesses rarely make a lot of money straight away. Your business may be very profitable, but you will almost certainly be ploughing a lot of those profits straight back in again, especially in the early days. The family will have to understand and accept that you may not be able to buy as many things – clothes, toys, holidays, etc – as you used to. Your financial position will hopefully improve as the business becomes established, but it is important that nobody in the family has unrealistic expectations at the outset.

Lack of security

The most worrying aspect of becoming self-employed is the loss of that regular wage with which you can pay the mortgage and the bills each month. For the first two or three years of a new small business your regular income may be very unreliable. If the business goes through a bad patch, perhaps through lack of orders, and costs have to be cut, the proprietor's drawings are always amongst the easiest expenses to reduce or even stop altogether until the crisis is over. This is painting a pessimistic picture, but you must discuss how the family would cope if the worst did happen. Would it be possible for someone else in the family (wife or husband) to have a job so that you had a regular income to fall back on? It is also vital to draw up a family budget to discover just what is the absolute minimum amount of money per week or month that you need to keep body and soul, and the mortgage, together. If you can be fairly confident that you can at least cover your absolute minimum living costs by one means or another it will help you and your family to feel a lot more secure during the difficult early years of dependency on your business.

Don't forget that your family can be a wonderful source of moral support and practical help if they are 100 per cent behind you. If they are not aware of all the possible implications of starting a business it may well lead to stress and tension. It might even wreck your marriage. The support of the family is one of the most important factors in the success of a new business.

Skills and knowledge

Skills and knowledge necessary to run a business

1 Selling ability. To sell yourself and your product effectively you will have to learn to deal with all kinds of people, from the angry customer to a potential distributor. They must be made to believe in you, in your competence, in the quality of your product and in your ability to succeed. In short you have to gain their trust. To do this you must demonstrate that you have the confidence in yourself, your abilities and your product or service.

Are salesmen born or bred? It's a little of both. Don't feel dismayed if you don't consider yourself to be a salesman. There are ways of improving techniques and developing your effectiveness at selling. These will be discussed later.

2 Organizational skills. The ability to organize your own time (and the time of others if you are going to employ staff) will be critical in the early days of a new business because you will always have too much to do. You must be a self-motivator, able to set yourself goals and keep yourself going when there is no one else driving you on. You need to be efficient, well organized, and you must hate to waste time.

3 Financial skills. The financial skills you will need as a businessman will involve *knowing what your financial position is now;* and *predicting what it will be in the near future.* The former merely involves regular, methodical book-keeping, not a skill that you are likely to possess before you have a business but one which most people can easily learn. The latter involves learning new techniques, which we will cover in Chapter 11. Financial planning is probably more difficult than book-keeping, and is certainly more time-consuming, which is why it is often neglected by the small business. But to master these techniques you need to have no skills other than competence in basic arithmetic.

4 Negotiating skills. Negotiating skills are extremely important to the owner of a small business. They are crucial for dealing with staff, suppliers, customers, professional advisers and a whole army of officials. Negotiating skills are probably more dependent on your innate personal characteristics than any of the skills we have looked at so far. The art of negotiating for the small businessman is a delicate blend of two contrasting abilities:

a the ability to be nice to people and to keep on friendly terms
b the ability to doggedly stand up for your own interests

The second ability is certainly the more important one, but the real challenge is to staunchly defend your own interests without ruining your good relations with people.

5 Paperwork. If you start your own business there will be a lot of forms to fill in, a lot of letters to read and reply to, a lot of bills to pay and, hopefully, a lot of invoices to send out to customers. If this kind of thing is not your strong point you cannot rely on simply 'muddling through'. You need to decide how you will best tackle your paperwork before you start your business. Will you teach yourself, attend a course, employ someone, or could another member of your family do it? A business which neglects its paperwork will be at best much less profitable than it should be, and at worst on a short cut to disaster.

The ability to write a good letter and to put together a written report when necessary, for example, to support an application for a bank loan or a grant, would also be very useful. Typing skills would be an added bonus. True, you can pay people to do these things for you but the kind of consultant who can also write a good report for you does not come cheap. There may be times when you don't even have enough cash to have your own report typed out. In other words, you are often forced to adopt the do-it-yourself approach in the early days, so you need many varied skills.

6 Emotional control. Another ability which is difficult to get just right. On the one hand you have to be ambitious, always striving for success. You have to be pretty ruthless at defending your own interests and not letting anyone get the better of you. However, if you go too far with these things you will end up losing your temper, behaving irrationally, and suffering from stress. Stress can lead to depression and to a very unsuccessful business. Ideally you have to be the kind of person who can motivate himself to go the extra mile, fight resolutely for his interests and strive continuously for success – without getting up tight – and that's not always easy!

7 Health and fitness. To cope physically and mentally with the demands of running a business you will have to be extremely healthy and fit, and you will have to stay that way!

If your health is not all that good you should consider very carefully whether starting a business really is the best thing for you to do. You should certainly consult your doctor. There would be three main causes for concern:

1 Would the stresses and strains of running a business make your health worse?

2 What would happen to the business if you were too ill to work for a week or two? Would there be someone else who could take over? If not, what would happen to your customers? Would they take their business elsewhere?

3 How would you manage financially? Remember that you do not receive sick pay if you are self-employed. You would just have to pay yourself for doing nothing. Where would this money come from?

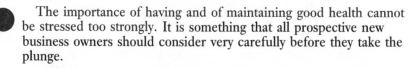 The importance of having and of maintaining good health cannot be stressed too strongly. It is something that all prospective new business owners should consider very carefully before they take the plunge.

Evaluating your skills and knowledge

We have identified seven important areas of skill or ability that would be critical factors for the success of a new business. It is often said that people planning to start a business should ask someone who knows them very well to assess them on these factors. You may be lucky enough to find someone who can do this properly but it is a very difficult position to put somebody in. So you will probably have to rely on your own ability to confront the realities of your own strengths and weaknesses. The important thing at this stage is to recognize where your weaknesses lie and decide what you are going to do about them.

Facing up to your weaknesses

A good businessman will devote a lot of effort to overcoming his areas of weakness or may take other measures to minimize their consequences. You may consider employing a specialist, finding a partner or training yourself to perform better in that area of weakness. All of these options will be covered in later chapters of this book.

● Weaknesses become problems only if you try to ignore them: you should recognize your weaknesses and resolve to overcome them.

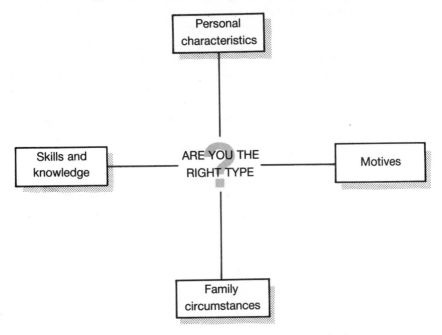

Fig 1.1 Key areas you should assess when thinking of starting your own business

Summary

1 There is no single model of a successful businessman, but some personal characteristics are more appropriate to running a business than others. Successful businessmen are often ambitious and ruthless workaholics who thrive on responsibility and hate wasting time.

2 Good motives for starting a business include a strong ambition to achieve certain goals, the desire to be able to make your own decisions and take the responsibility for them, and a firm belief that you have an idea which is a commercial winner. Less acceptable reasons for starting your own business would be a desire to escape from your current job or the belief that starting a business would be a quick, easy or reliable way to make a lot of money.

3 Starting a business may bring difficulties to your family life since it can often result in a reduction in money, security and leisure time. The best way to minimize the effects of these problems is to ensure that the family understands and accepts all the implications of starting a business.

4 Strengths which are important to the running of a small business include selling skills, organizational ability, financial and negotiating skills, the ability to cope with all the paperwork, plus confidence in your own emotional control and health. Since nobody is perfect in all these areas, perhaps the most important strengths are the ability to recognize your areas of weakness and the determination to overcome them.

2 Is it a good idea?

Aims of this chapter

The objective of this chapter is to offer some guidelines for picking the 'commercial winner' mentioned in Chapter 1. Even if you already have a business idea it is important to go through the whole of this chapter in an open-minded way and examine the three steps you must go through to arrive at the right business idea. They are:

- Idea generation
- Idea selection
- Idea evaluation

Idea generation

Many people have a long held ambition to start a business and be their own boss. They like the concept of running a business, the lifestyle, the achievement factor, but they have no particular leanings towards any one type of business. If you are one of these people, don't worry, for you are one of many. The first stage of starting a new business follows the same process that existing businesses (including large multi-national corporations) go through when they want to bring out a new product. It is called **idea generation**. There are three methods you could use to help you develop a healthy list containing a variety of business ideas.

The 'Ideas Book'

Many people consider the idea of starting a business for a long time before they actually take the plunge. During this time most of them will think of a multitude of ideas for new businesses, many of which will be forgotten forever within a few days. If you are in the position of having some time to wait before you can realistically start a business it would pay you to keep an 'Ideas Book'. Quite simply this involves jotting down a brief outline of any good business ideas that occur to you. Over time, say six months to a year, you could build up a considerable number of ideas for a new business, some of which would be better than others. You should make notes outlining the details of all the ideas, because when you read through them all again a few months later you will be surprised how much your views on some of them will have changed. A brainwave which you have in the bath one evening in August may not seem to be such a sensible idea in the cold light of day in the middle of January. Reading through your 'Ideas Book' will often spark off new ideas, or at least improvements to existing ones.

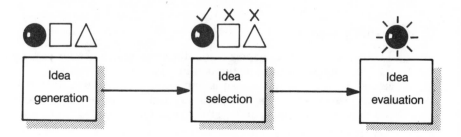

Fig. 2.1 Three steps to choosing the right business idea

'Ideas' publications

There are a number of magazines and other publications which you could read as a source of business ideas. You can often find this type of magazine on the shelves of the larger newsagents or you could try the public library where you might also find back copies. There are many to choose from, but three particular examples will now be described.

1 Exchange and Mart. This well-known weekly small ads paper has the twin advantages of being cheap and readily available at most newsagents. The whole thing is a wealth of small business information. You might develop ideas from the kind of products and services that other people are advertising, and later on it may be a useful source for assessing some of your competitors (by sending off for their leaflets) and could help you find suppliers. It also contains a 'business opportunities' section in which people advertise their own business ideas and offer them for sale. However, most of these must be treated very cautiously. The more extravagant the advertiser's claim, the less it is likely to have any substance.

2 Business Success. At £1.75 per copy, the monthly magazine *Business Success* is more expensive but also more sophisticated. It is normally available at the larger newsagents such as WH Smith. It has a business ideas section containing details of ideas that people are trying to sell, often for quite a low price. Again, these kinds of deals need to be treated with the utmost caution. However, you don't have to actually follow up any of the adverts, you could just use the magazine itself as a source of ideas. It also contains very extensive details about franchising, usually with at least one case study of a franchise in operation each month. You will also find informative articles about more general business issues.

3 Subscribing to a business publication. A better but more expensive alternative is to consider subscribing to a 'business ideas' publication. The Institute of Small Businesses publishes a quarterly magazine called *Business Opportunities Digest* which contains a large number of interesting and stimulating ideas, case histories and other articles. The Institute also offers members various advisory services. The *Digest* comes free to members, but membership does cost £59.95 per annum, although the Institute sometimes runs a special offer which entitles new members to a first year fee of £39.95. If you would like more details of the Institute of Small Businesses you should write to:

The Institute of Small Businesses, 11 Bloomfield St, London EC2M 7AY.

Systematic market analysis

This is the kind of activity that large companies with market research departments engage in as a method of generating ideas for new products or new business activities. The individual person hoping to start a business can clearly not go to the same lengths as a professional market researcher but can make use of some of the same techniques as a means of developing a more systematic and efficient way of generating new business ideas. There are a number of independent market research companies which make money by employing a large staff of professional researchers to investigate market trends. The research findings are then published as reports which are available for purchase to anybody who wants them. Unfortunately they are usually very expensive and well beyond the budget of the small businessman. You can, however, get hold of them in some of the larger commercial libraries.

If you talk to the librarians and explain your requirements they may well unearth a number of sources of published information for you. It is well worth remembering that librarians are trained to know where to find information and that it's one of the cardinal rules of business to make full use of the experts – especially when they are free!

However, you should be wise to two cautionary notes about the practicality of using these published sources of market information:

1 **Accessibility.** Unless you live in a large city you may find it difficult to gain sight of these reports. Due to their high cost they are being stocked by fewer and fewer libraries. You should find them in the central reference library in a large city, or at your nearest university or polytechnic (where there may be a small fee for non-students).

2 **Applicability.** You have to ask yourself whether the reports are truly applicable to your situation. They will tend to cover general trends in fairly large national markets; and reports on consumer markets will be much easier to find than those covering business-to-business markets. Small businesses are usually concerned with a much more specialized sector of the market. This may not invalidate these reports as sources of ideas but it does mean that you have to be prepared to undertake some additional research into your specialized part of the market.

You will find details of all sources of market information of relevance to small businesses in the companion volume *Successful Marketing for Small Businesses*, together with advice on how to research your own specialized market.

Idea selection

Let's be clear about the objectives of this stage of the process of choosing your business idea. When you are examining the 1001 business ideas that you have thought up you should be asking yourself:

1 How suitable is that kind of business for me?
2 How feasible is it for me to start that kind of business?
3 How good would I be at running a business like that?
4 Do I have any knowledge of the trade?
5 Would a business like that make full use of my strengths?
6 Would my weaknesses be a severe handicap in that kind of business?

Since much of the performance of your business will depend on you it is essential to select a business where you will already have a lot of advantages and the minimum number of disadvantages. If you are going to beat the competition you will have to be better at it than them. So you need to choose a field in which you have real expertise. You should want to end up with three ideas that you have selected by the end of this section, each one of which you would feel personally happy and confident about starting as a business. How should you go about doing this?

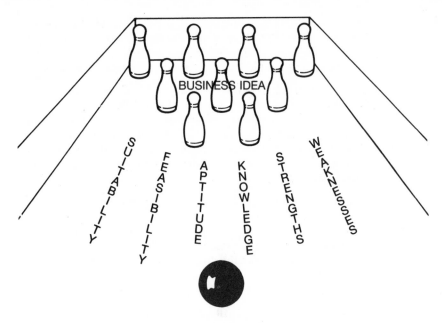

Fig. 2.2 Idea selection

Initial screening

If you have a reasonably lengthy list of ideas at this stage, it is a good idea to reduce them fairly quickly to a more manageable list of no more than ten ideas. To achieve this it is only realistic to give each idea a quick subjective assessment along the following lines:

Idea Screening Process

1 Would I like to run this business?

2 Would I be able to run this business?

3 Would I have the money to start this business?

The Idea Selection Matrix

Once you have narrowed things down to a reasonable number of business ideas you can use the 'Idea Selection Matrix' (fig. 2.3) to help you to work out which of those ideas is most compatible with your own strengths and expertise. Simply give each idea a mark out of ten for how well it conforms to each of the criteria listed in the left hand column of the table. Before beginning this task let's run through the criteria to see exactly what is meant by each one.

1 **Family commitments.** How compatible with your family commitments is the business idea? If you are 'young, free and

single' you will probably be able to give ten out of ten for almost every idea. If, on the other hand, you have young children there may be much more of a problem, particularly with businesses that could make fluctuating and unpredictable demands on your time.

2 Time involved. Whether or not you have family commitments you will have to assess the amount of time which you would need to devote to your business and give marks out of ten according to how easy it would be for you to find that much time. This could be a particularly acute problem for you if you are going to start your business on a part-time basis initially in conjunction with your full-time job.

3 Suitable premises. The critical question here is how easy would it be to house each of your businesses in suitable premises. If you plan to start on a part-time basis from home, the suitability of your home as the business premises would be a crucial factor. Even if you plan to start full-time from other premises, the availability of suitable premises will be more problematical for some types of business than for others (see Chapter 6).

4 Capital requirement. All businesses cost something to start up (Chapter 11 goes into more detail on starting up costs). You must have a very rough idea of the capital requirements for the business ideas on your list, and you can award marks out of ten for how closely this matches up with the amount of money that you would *like* to invest in your business. (*NB* This is not the same thing as the maximum amount of money which you *could*, if necessary, invest in your business.) For example, someone who has received £10,000 redundancy pay may prefer to invest half that amount and use the other half for savings or for some special family purchases, but could, if absolutely necessary, invest up to £10,000 in a business. He would therefore give ten out of ten to a business with start-up costs of about £5000, five out of ten to a business requiring start-up capital of £7500 and nothing out of ten for a business needing anything over £10,000.

5 Product expertise. This refers to the expert technical or trade knowledge of the particular product or service that forms the central core of your business idea. How much do you really know about it? If you plan to continue on a self-employed basis a trade which you have been practising as an employee for many years then there should be no problem. But what if you have been in the trade, but all your experience has been in sales? Do you really know how to 'make' the product? Even if you are planning to take on specialist staff from the start, the boss of a small business should know exactly what's supposed to happen on the shop floor. If it's a hobby-into-business idea you may be on even trickier ground. You may know all about the hobby as a dedicated amateur, but do you know anything about it from the trade point of view?

If your product knowledge really is weak it cannot be stressed too strongly how valuable it would be to get a job on the 'inside' for a short time. You should look on it as an investment – and it could be the best one you'll ever make.

Back to the Idea Selection Matrix. If you don't have experience of the trade in question you must award yourself very low marks – there's no point in pretending! However, you could raise the marks slightly if you know that you could gain practical experience in that business because you already have connections in the trade, e.g. relatives or friends in the same business who would let you work for them for a short time, or at least let you watch and pass tips on to you.

Selection criteria	Business ideas									
	1	2	3	4	5	6	7	8	9	10
Family commitments										
Time involved										
Suitable premises										
Capital requirement										
Product expertise										
Business skills										
Market knowledge										
Personal preference										
Total score (out of 80)										

Fig. 2.3 The Idea Selection Matrix

6 **Business skills.** What kind of skills would be required to manage each kind of business on your list? For example, would there be a lot of selling involved, would most of it be organizing

production, would it be mainly design work? And would they conform to your personal strengths which you identified in Chapter 1, or would they depend alarmingly on some of your weaker characteristics?

7 Market knowledge. In some instances market knowledge is even more important than product knowledge. Would you know where and how to get sales for each idea? Would you know about the competition in the market, how they operated, what their products and prices were? Would you know much about the customers, what they were like, what their preferences were?

8 Personal preference. Last but not least, would you actually like to spend your time running each particular business? Any business concept which would not give you personal pleasure and satisfaction would not be a good idea. However, note that personal preference is only one of eight relevant criteria for idea selection, and that's much more realistic than the overwhelming importance given to it by many budding entrepreneurs. It's no good basing a business on an activity or a hobby that you enjoy if it scores very low on all the other important criteria. It won't be an activity you enjoy for long if your business becomes a battle for survival!

Idea evaluation

The previous section was all about selecting the business idea which is most compatible with your existing personal strengths and circumstances. The idea which scored most highly should be the one which you would make the best job of starting up and running. This is very important, because in a small business so much depends on the personal strengths and weaknesses, the *effectiveness*, of the owner. But it is still not the whole story. However efficiently some businesses are run they would still fail to be profitable in the market place as it is no use having a business which you are ideally suited to if its purpose is to make a product that hardly anybody wants to buy. In this section we must therefore examine your business using a completely different set of criteria. These criteria have nothing to do with your personal abilities. They are about the market place, the competition, the demand for your product or service, and the viability of your idea.

There is a tendency amongst new businesses to display excessive confidence in their business idea. Quite naturally, people tend to be very enthusiastic, very optimistic and simply want to get the business going as quickly as possible. Remarks such as these are often heard:

'It's sheer genius', 'It can't fail', and 'I can't understand why nobody's done it before'.

Unfortunately, ideas that are sheer genius can still fail and there may be many good reasons why nobody's done it before! In the market place the customer is king and if the customer does not rate your product or service as highly as you do, then the business has, at best, an extremely difficult task ahead.

Market research

Large companies minimize this problem by carrying out extensive market research before they launch a new product. Small businessmen tend to assume that they don't have the resources to undertake market research, but this is not necessarily so. It is true that they are unlikely to be able to afford the services of an independent market research company, but they can make use of some very effective do-it-yourself market research techniques which will require quite a lot of time but relatively little money. The time will be time well spent if it results in a real market winner. More importantly, it will certainly help to avoid the making of the fatal mistake of backing a hunch which turns out to have no prospect in the market place. This section will examine some of these market research techniques.

The Idea Evaluation Matrix

The Idea Evaluation Matrix is shown on page 31. It's just the same as the Selection Matrix apart from the variables down the left hand side. What we are aiming to achieve in this section is a set of guidelines concerning the market opportunity for your business ideas. You may want to carry out this exercise for the top five ideas identified by your Idea Selection Matrix.

1 **Market demand.** In other words, is there a good market for your product or service? This question requires a lot of investigation. In fact, because the level of market demand will be so important in the success of a new business, this criterion has been split into three separate indicators. You must give each idea a score out of ten for each of the indicators. In this way, the level of demand is allocated a total of 30 points which reflects its importance in evaluating your business idea.

Personal and subjective view. The first indicator is your own personal conviction that there is a healthy demand for this product or service. You could call this a hunch. It's not based on any objective evidence that you could prove. You have to be aware of the advantages and disadvantages of hunches. On the one hand you have to have the confidence to back your own beliefs, and some of the most successful entrepreneurs have made it by backing their own judgments, sometimes against professional advice. On the other hand, many more new businesses have failed because their owners have followed hunches without careful consideration of all the implications. So your own beliefs about the demand for the product or service should form a part of the evaluation process, but only *one* part. There are other criteria which must also be used.

Opinions of others. It is very useful to ask around to see if other people share your belief that there is widespread demand for your product or service. You could ask relatives, close friends, colleagues at work, or people in the pub. You could even undertake a survey of people you don't know at all, either in the street, or by knocking on their doors. In the long run it will be all these other people who make up the market for your product or service so you need to find out whether they like it as much as you do. But, you really must ensure that you test the opinions of people who might conceivably be future buyers of your product. For example, if your idea involved the manufacture of some kind of baby equipment it would be foolish to canvas the views of old or unmarried people. Once you have a reasonable number of opinions you should be able to devise a scoring system and give a value to these opinions in an overall mark out of ten.

Objective evidence. People like bank managers, accountants or advisers at Enterprise Agencies, who have a very wide knowledge of the local market, would be able to give you a more objective assessment of the level of demand. Opinions from wholesalers and retailers would be valuable because they come into contact with so many of the potential users of your product, and know what kind of things they buy. It is very difficult and can be very time-consuming to assess the level of demand for your product or service in this way, but the information you can gain really is so valuable that it is vital to make the effort. Once again you must compare the responses you get and come up with an average mark out of ten for each business idea. Your local library should be able to help you to identify any relevant journals and reports.

2 **Market growth.** It is obviously preferable to be operating in a growing market. For example, the fast food take away market has been growing very quickly, and the market for traditional fish and chips has been declining.

The faster the market is growing the more marks you should award the idea. An expanding market has room for new companies, but a static or declining market would be very difficult for a new company to enter. Prices tend to be forced down and profits are very hard to make, and the advantages would almost certainly lie with the established firms. There just would not be enough customers to go round. In a growth market there are new customers or people are simply consuming more. Existing firms often can't keep up with the growing demand. Prices and therefore profits tend to be higher because customers are chasing goods rather than producers all chasing the same customers, so a new firm finds it much easier to enter the market.

Trade journals, published market research reports and people in the trade are very useful sources of information about market growth.

3 Market accessibility. Market accessibility is all about how easy it is for you to reach your market, to make your product available for customers to buy and to make it easy for them to buy it. How easy would it be for you to communicate with potential customers so that they will know your firm exists, what it offers and how they can place an order? If you are going to provide a basic service, say domestic electrical repairs, in a restricted local area you could score very highly here. Even if you can't afford to advertise in local newspapers you could put a leaflet through every letterbox and could follow it up with a personal call. If your business idea relies on winning customers over a much wider area, perhaps regionally or even nationally, you must ask yourself how easy it will be to make those customers aware that you exist and then to go further and convince them that they should try your product.

4 Competition. The basic question here is 'how much competition would there be in this market?' This is really two questions. Firstly, would there be a lot of competitors? Secondly, how strong would those competitors be? The stronger the competition, in number and/or in strength, the lower the score of a business idea along similar lines.

5 Market niche. A 'niche' is the word given to a tiny part of a market where the customers want something clearly distinct from the mainstream product or service in that market. For example, in the fast food business it would be very difficult for a new small business with one outlet to compete successfully with an established giant like McDonalds or Wimpy. Their economies of scale make it possible for them to combine a popular product with a high level of service, in attractive premises right in the city centre, and all at a reasonable price. It is very unlikely that a small business trying to compete directly in the same market could offer customers such an attractive overall package. However, a new small business, maybe with smaller, less expensive premises and slightly off the beaten track, could probably make a good profit out of a very small share of that fast food market. It would therefore make a lot of sense to

offer something that was different from McDonalds and Wimpy, and more closely matching the preferences of a small but identifiable group of fast food customers. This might, for example, be a take away which serves only additive-free foods and places an onus on healthy eating. By exploiting this niche in the market, a new small business could take advantage of a growth market whilst at the same time avoiding direct competition with the larger companies in that market. An idea which recognizes and takes advantage of a niche scores highly on the matrix.

6 Price levels. This aims to discover whether prices charged by companies already operating in the market are high relative to costs (in which case profitability will be good), or whether prices are low (in which case profitability could be low or even negative). You may have worked out some accurate costings of your own to establish the cost of manufacturing a particular product or providing a service. If you know how much existing companies are charging, you can estimate their profitability. However, beware if you do not have a good inside knowledge of the industry. You may be underestimating the costs and therefore overestimating the profitability.

To have your ideas confirmed you could show your figures to someone who has a better knowlege of the business than you have. Ideally this would be somebody who already works in a similar line of business.

In the long run pricing and profit margins are extremely important. There's no point having a business if you are not going to make a satisfactory amount of money out of it. So you should award high marks out of ten for ideas concerning markets where prices and profit margins appear to be good, very low marks out of ten if prices and profit margins look to be poor.

7 Consistency of demand. Will sales in your potential line of business be regular, or will they be seasonal, up and down, or subject to other outside influences? If demand will be irregular, would you be able to cope in busy times and survive during the slack times? When business is very slack, the longer established firms will have reserves to see them through, but a new business might encounter severe cash flow problems if sales suddenly fall off. Dependency on one large customer could also leave you vulnerable in a similar way.

8 Potential customers. Have you got any? If you could start this business tomorrow would you have any customers, any definite sales? Has anyone given you a firm promise of an order? Whilst evaluating your business idea you should have spoken to a lot of people, including individuals who could be potential customers, as well as trade people who could be much larger customers. Rather than just expressing approval of your scheme (which could just be politeness on their part), did any show genuine enthusiasm, and 'above all did any of them make you promise to contact them as soon as you were in business so that they could place an order? This is a very good test of whether an idea really does have promise and is reflected in a high mark on the matrix.

Selection criteria		Business ideas				
		1	2	3	4	5
Market demand	*Personal and subjective view*					
	Opinions of others					
	Objective evidence					
Market growth						
Market accessibility						
Competition						
Market niche						
Price levels						
Consistency of demand						
Potential customers						
Total score (*out of 100*)						

Fig. 2.4 The Idea Evaluation Matrix

The business idea

If the same idea scored highest in both the Selection Matrix and the Evaluation Matrix you are very fortunate and your search for a business idea is over. If your favourite personal idea scored low on the market evaluation then you are faced with a much more difficult choice. It is very heartbreaking to abandon an idea that you have cherished for years, but it is better to abandon it now rather than start the business and see it fail later. Going back to

Chapter 1, consider what the successful entrepreneur would do. No doubt about it, he would be ruthless, forget sentimentality and choose the market winner.

Summary

There are a number of steps in the selection of a good business idea.

1 It is advisable to devote some time to thinking up a number of alternative business ideas to compare against each other rather than simply pressing ahead with one single idea – the idea generation stage.

2 The first set of criteria against which you should judge each business idea is its compatibility with your own personal strengths – the idea selection stage.

3 The second set of evaluative criteria involves an attempt to assess the commercial viability of each business idea – the idea evaluation stage.

4 To maximize the changes of success for your new business you need to find an idea which scores highly at both the selection and evaluation stages.

From this point onwards this book will assume that you have a definite business idea and will concentrate on the steps that you should take from now on to develop that idea and turn it into a real business.

3 Ownership

Aims of this chapter

It is the objective of this chapter to help you to choose the form of business ownership that would be most suitable for you. It will examine the four main alternative forms of business ownership, explain what each one means and discuss the advantages and disadvantages of each.

The four main possibilities open to new businesses are:

- Sole trader
- Partnership
- Limited company
- Workers' cooperative

We will also look at a slightly different form of business, **the franchise**. A franchise is not a different form of business ownership. If you buy a franchise you would still have to decide which of the above forms of business ownership would be best for you. However, a franchise is certainly a different way of starting and running a business, and one that is growing in popularity. A latter section of this chapter will therefore explain what franchising is, look at the pros and cons, and raise a few points of interest to prospective franchisees.

Having chosen your form of business ownership, you will have to finalise the name of the business, so the last section of this chapter explains the regulations concerning business names.

Sole trader

This is by far the least complicated form of business ownership. The main features are now summarized.

Sole trader – the facts

1 A sole trader is classed as a self-employed person.

2 An individual owns the business – there are no partners.

3 There is no limit on the size the business can grow to or the number of people it can employ.

4 Legally the business and its owner are inseparable. This means:

  a the business is taxed in the same way as an individual, through income tax *b* the owner must pay self-employed National Insurance contributions

Rates of taxation and national insurance may change annually, but details of the current situation can be found in leaflet IR 56, 'Employed or Self-employed', obtainable from your local Inland Revenue office.

c the owner and the business being one and the same person, the owner has unlimited liability for all the debts of the business

5 Almost all business expenses can be offset against the trader's tax bill, but not against National Insurance contributions.

6 There are no legal procedures that must be followed to set up as a sole trader.

7 A sole trader must still comply with all the laws of the land which affect businesses, e.g. laws concerning VAT, employment of staff, health and safety, planning permission.

There are both advantages and disadvantages to life as a sole trader.

Sole trader – the advantages

1 **Few legal formalities.** Apart from conforming to the general laws and regulations which apply to all businesses there is nothing special that you need to do to start up as a sole trader; no forms to fill in, no agreements to work out, no elaborate procedures to follow. Apart from saving time and making life easier it also saves you a lot of money on your start-up costs. Other forms of business ownership can involve legal and/or accountancy fees before you have even started trading. Most new businesses are relatively small scale enterprises, and set up with very limited funds. That limited investment must be put to the most productive use possible, therefore most new businesses will not find it in their best interests to allocate a valuable proportion of their scarce start-up capital to non-productive legal expenses.

2 **Financial advantages.** *a Lower taxation.* Most small new businesses, which have a relatively low turnover and profit at first, will pay less tax as a sole trader (or a partnership) than they would as a limited company. For larger scale enterprises this may not be the case. If you expect to have a high initial turnover and to grow rapidly you should consult an accountant about your most tax efficient form of business ownership.

b Longer to pay taxes. As a self-employed sole trader you will pay very little tax in the early years of trading as your business establishes itself. Once you have completed your first year's trading and the accountant has examined your books he will send a tax return to the Inland Revenue on your behalf. The Inland Revenue will then send a bill for the taxes you owe. By this time you could have already been trading for the best part of two years. You will then be given time to pay these taxes, in two instalments, the following January and July. It is therefore quite common for new businesses trading as sole traders or partnerships not to pay any tax until two or even three years after they have started trading. Of course, you don't avoid paying the taxes, you only postpone it. In the early days of trading however, many new businesses are short of cash, and need to retain within the business every penny they can for working capital. Having a two or three year breathing space before you pay your first tax bill enables the business to establish itself and to build up sales and profitability, so that by the time you do have to pay your first tax bill it should be easier for you to take that kind of money out of the business. It is important, however, to budget for any taxes you may have to pay in the future.

c Lower accountancy fees. Just as the sole trader is the simplest form of business to set up, it is also the most straightforward type of business to control as far as the book-keeping and annual accounts are concerned. The less time an accountant has to spend on the business's accounts the lower his fees will be.

3 **Independence.** As a sole trader, apart from obeying the law you are answerable to nobody but yourself. You make all the decisions and have complete control of the business. One of the attractions of forming a business for many people is exactly this kind of independence.

Sole trader – the disadvantages

1 **Unlimited liability.** In the eyes of the law and for tax purposes your business and yourself are viewed as an inseperable entity. You may call the business by your own name: 'Fred Bloggs (Plumber)', or you may give it a completely different name: 'Round the Clock Plumbing Services'. It makes no difference to the legal position, you and the business are one and the same. This means that if 'Round the Clock Plumbing Services' orders supplies on credit, it is you, Fred Bloggs, who is responsible for paying. If 'Round the Clock Plumbing Services' found itself in a real mess, owing a lot of money and ending up being taken to court by its suppliers, the bank, the landlord or any other creditors it would be Fred Bloggs personally who would be in court facing the angry creditors and Fred personally who would be responsible for paying the money

back. As a sole trader, all the business's money belongs to Fred and all Fred's money to the business. The court would therefore be entitled to seize all Fred's personal assets in order to pay the debts of 'Round the Clock Plumbing Services'. If all the assets of 'Round the Clock Plumbing Services' and of Fred were put together and were still not enough to pay off all the debts of the business, then Fred would be declared personally bankrupt and would be banned from owning a business again for at least two years. Taken to its ultimate conclusion, this is the meaning of the term **unlimited liability.** All sole traders have unlimited liability for the debts of the business.

2 Going-it-alone. Many people would say that the biggest drawback of being a sole trader is the fact that you're on your own with only your own strengths, expertise, capital, and energy to rely on. If you fall short in any one area, the business may end up in trouble. However, this disadvantage would apply to a limited company with only one owner just as much as its applies to a sole trader. Specific disadvantages of going-it-alone include:

a Limited capital. Other things being equal, one person going into business on his own is going to have less personal capital to invest to get that business going than three or four people who join together to start a business.

b Limited expertise. This can be a more difficult problem for the sole trader to overcome. It can be very difficult and time-consuming to gain expertise and develop strengths which you lack. The ideal partnership is one which brings together people with different strengths, for example, a production/technical expert with a partner whose main strength is in selling.

However, as will be explained later, partnerships do have some severe disadvantages, and many people are justifiably reluctant to become involved in a partnership even to gain some real business expertise which they lack. So what alternative methods are available for a sole trader to make up for his own weaknesses or lack of business expertise? There are a number of possibilities which will be examined in later chapters of this book, including improving your own expertise (Chapter 5), employing specialist staff (Chapter 9), and hiring outside professionals (Chapter 5).

c Limited time. The third drawback of going-it-alone for small new businesses is the great shortage of time that you will face. A partner could share the workload, but alternatives might include taking on a part-time secretary and asking family and friends to help out in the early days. There is usually a lot of goodwill shown towards a new business venture and people will often be only too pleased to help out. You can also put in the hours yourself!

d Loneliness. Being a sole trader can sometimes feel like a journey along a very long, hard road. It can be very lonely. Some people love the independence and responsibility of being in sole command all the time, but others value the opportunity to share decision making at times and to have some support to call on when difficult decisions are required. These feelings can sometimes make a partner seem to be a very attractive proposition.

So what are the alternatives? Family support can be of great value as can the confidence of close friends. A strong relationship with other small businesses can be most helpful, either neighbouring businesses or perhaps business owners that you could meet at a Small Business Club. The community spirit in large multi-tenancy premises like managed workshops (see Chapter 6) can also be very helpful to sole traders.

3 The vulnerability of the sole trader. In addition to the potential risks of unlimited liability and of going-it-alone the self-employed owner-manager can be vulnerable and insecure in a number of other ways:

a Health. Many sole traders are much too vulnerable to the effects of ill health. As a sole trader you need to consider the consequences of a serious illness or an accident which might prevent you from working for some time. In particular you need to be able to answer two important questions:

1 Where would your income come from if you could not work?

2 How would the business be kept going if you could not work?

As regards the first question, it is important to remember that as a self-employed person you would be entitled only to supplementary benefit if you had no income. So it may be that you would need to take out an insurance policy to provide your family with sufficient income if you were too ill to work.

The second question is a trickier one. It would depend very much on the size of the business. If the business has a number of employees one of them can be earmarked 'the stand-in gaffer' for such occasions and can be trained sufficiently well beforehand to carry out the task, maybe with some periodic supervision from a member of your family or a close friend. However, a very small business with no permanent staff or maybe just a couple of young, inexperienced employees, could face a major problem. Unless somebody, for instance, a member of the family, could virtually take over your role, it may be necessary to lay off the staff and put the business into virtual hibernation while you are sick. In these circumstances, how long could the business continue to meet its overheads? You could take out a 'loss of profits' insurance policy, but not all small businesses can afford so much insurance cover.

Insurance is covered in more detail in Chapter 7, but it should be noted that premiums for such policies can be quite high.

b Holidays. Holidays present the sole trader with exactly the same problem as sickness, but the important difference is that they can be planned ahead. It is common for small businesses to have a holiday closure period, perhaps one week at Christmas and two weeks in the summer when all the staff are on holiday. Customers and suppliers are informed in advance of the closure dates and the business simply shuts up shop. This arrangement is not always feasible, however. Some businesses would lose too much goodwill if they were unwilling to serve their customers for a period as long as, say, two weeks. It is therefore very common for sole traders not to have holidays – a state of affairs which does not always go down very well with their families!

c Panics! As a sole trader you are more likely to have 'mad panics' when things don't go according to plan, and when they do occur they will be all the more difficult to handle if you are on your own. What follows could happen to you!

John Trader's panic!

John is getting himself into a fine pickle with two important orders to get out, both of which are behind schedule, and, as if that isn't enough, his wife is due to have a baby imminently and that is making him even more edgy. He then discovers that an employee has made a serious error with one of the orders which could take days to put right. John kicks himself hard. He knew all along he should have done that job himself! He's very worried that he'll end up losing that customer now. Still reeling from the shock of the employee's blunder, John receives a phone call from the Customs and Excise who want to arrange an appointment for the VAT Inspector to make a visit to look over the firm's books sometime the following week. Unfortunately, the book-keeping has suffered due to the pressure of meeting orders, and the books are now about three months behind! How on earth is John going to manage?

Not a happy prospect, but many small firms would recognize that this is not a ridiculously far-fetched story. This kind of thing could, and from time to time does, happen to small over-stretched businesses. In a partnership situation, one partner could concentrate on getting the books up-to-date while the other partner worked on rectifying the production problem. And if John's wife decided to give birth in the middle of it all, at least his partner would still be there to keep things going.

If our friend John Trader was on his own it would be a real headache, to say the least. He would probably pull through it somehow, but his family life would no doubt suffer, his relations with at least one of those customers would probably be damaged, and John would certainly have a few more grey hairs at the end of it all!

Sole trader – checklist

Is a sole trader the best form of business ownership for you? To help you to decide, read through the following checklist and tick the appropriate column. To how many of the questions could you honestly answer *yes*? If you have to answer *no* to more than two or three of them, you might find life very tough as a sole trader.

		Yes	No
1	Is independence and complete control of your business very important to you?		
2	Does the idea of sharing your profits with a partner bother you?		
3	Could you cope with the pressures of being a sole trader?		
4	Can your raise enough money yourself to start the business?		
5	Do you have the expertise/capability to run the business by yourself?		
6	Could you afford to employ someone, for example, a secretary or foreman, to help you?		
7	Could your business continue to function for a while if you were unavailable for work?		
8	Could your business shut down completely for holidays in the Summer and at Christmas?		
9	Are you as confident as you can be about being able to rely on continued good health?		
10	Can you think of at least three people from your family or close friends who would really be able to step in and give you a lot of help in an emergency?		

Sole trader – a summary

We can summarize the advantages and disadvantages of being a sole trader as follows:

Advantages	Disadvantages
1 Few legal formalities	1 Unlimited liability
2 Financial advantages:	2 Going-it-alone:
a lower taxation	*a* limited capital
b longer to pay taxes	*b* limited expertise
c lower accountancy fees	*c* limited time
3 Independence	*d* loneliness and crises at work
	e sickness and holidays

Partnership

If you are considering a partnership you should make sure you have read the sole trader section of this chapter thoroughly, because it clarifies many of the basic concepts involved in choosing the right form of business ownership.

A partnership is a firm which has two or more proprietors. All the partners share in the firm's profits, and each is individually responsible for all the firm's debts. For tax purposes, partners are treated as though they were sole traders. Partners have to pay self-employed National Insurance contributions at Class 2 and Class 4 rates, just like sole traders. The financial considerations are exactly the same as those of the sole trader. For example, most new small businesses will pay less tax as a partnership than they would as a limited company.

This section will cover the following points:

1 The disadvantages of forming a partnership.
2 Unlimited liability and partnerships.
3 The advantages of forming a partnership.
4 The partnership agreement.
5 Partnership insurance.
6 A trial period.

The disadvantages of forming a partnership

People often say that forming a partnership is just like getting married, except that it is easier to start but even more difficult to get out of it later on if you change your mind! You could also add that people are much more inclined to rush into partnerships than they are to rush into marriage. If partners do find that they no longer get on together and want to dissolve the partnership and split up the business, it will be a very difficult, lengthy and expensive procedure. If the partners can't agree to cooperate over the business any more, it is very unlikely that they will be able to reach an amicable agreement on how to divide up the business assets. Many perfectly viable businesses have been forced into liquidation as a direct result of partnerships splitting up.

Unfortunately the risk of a partnership ending in 'divorce' cannot be dismissed. Business partnerships can break up for many reasons.

1 **Effort.** It is very easy in a partnership situation for one partner to feel that he is working harder than the other(s). Resentment can grow like a cancer once it starts, culminating in the ridiculous situation where partners are deliberately working much less hard than they could: 'If Fred's only going to work at half-pace (or part-time) I'm damned if I'm going to kill myself working flat out (or working overtime)'. It sounds silly and childish but in a partnership these feelings can get out of hand precisely because there is so much more at stake. It's a danger that all partners should be aware of and should keep under control by talking together regularly and openly about each others' performance.

2 **Competence.** Partnerships are often formed because people have different strengths and areas of expertise. If one of the partners turns out to be somewhat less competent than expected in his area of responsibility it can create tensions within the partnership. If the partner with all the technical expertise keeps making expensive mistakes, what do you do? You can't give him the sack. It is vital to ensure beforehand that partners who are joining the business because they would bring a particular expertise, really are every bit as good as they say they are. Some kind of trial period of working together without forming a partnership may be the best way to assess this.

3 **Policy making.** Many partnerships are formed to exploit a specific business idea. As time passes, the idea evolves and the business develops and new policy decisions need to be agreed. It is at this stage that partners are likely to display different priorities. To minimize this risk it is vital to have a medium to long-term plan for future developments to ensure that all partners are still speaking the same language.

4 **Business ownership.** If you share your business idea with two other partners you would each be entitled to one third of the profits and would each own one third of the business. If it were your business idea originally would you be content to own only one third of the fruits of that idea, particularly if it turned out to be very successful? This is a very important question. All partners must be completely reconciled to their share of the business profits. Many partnership problems arise from a partner's dissatisfaction with his share of the proceeds. The long-term success of any partnership

depends crucially on each partner's continued willingness to accept the agreed distribution of the firm's profits.

Unlimited liability and partnerships

All the partners in a partnership are collectively and individually responsible for liabilities incurred by any member of the partnership.

Irresponsible Bob

Assume a partnership of four men, Jim, Fred, Bob and Dick. Assume also that one of them, Bob, is a little irresponsible where money is concerned: of his own money and the firm's money.

Bob's misdemeanours

1 Unlike the other three partners Bob has not been paying his income tax bills, which of course for partners, as for sole traders, have to be paid in a lump sum retrospectively.
2 Bob had also ordered some things for the business which were considered unnecessary and extravagant, in particular a suite of expensive office furniture and an inappropriate computer system.
3 Even worse, Bob has used the business name to order a number of items for personal consumption without the other partners having any knowledge whatsoever of the transactions. These items ranged from building alterations to a new car for his wife!

The point about these three different examples is that the other three partners are collectively responsible for the actions of irresponsible Bob. It does not matter if the other partners were totally unaware of Bob's actions, and it makes no difference if they received none of the benefits of those purchases. If Bob does not settle those debts, the other three partners are liable. **They are collectively responsible for Bob's liabilities if they were incurred in the name of the business.**

Unfortunately there's worse to come. **They are also individually responsible for Bob's debts.** Let's assume that Bob really had taken the other three for a ride and had run up debts of £50,000 before the situation came fully to light. What might happen then?

The consequences of Bob's misdemeanours

The partnership of Jim, Fred, Bob and Dick was not a business with a lot of assets, and it was well beyond the resources of the business to pay off Bob's debts of £50,000. In this situation the creditors are entitled to pursue each partner individually through the courts to recover their debts. Dick and Fred were not much use here. They had very little personal wealth, but it soon became apparent to the creditors and to the courts that Jim was quite well off. He had a house, and he had been left a reasonable sum of money fairly recently in the will of a relative. He had still not decided what to do with this money. The courts were to save him the trouble of making this decision. All Jim's personal assets were seized by the courts to pay off Bob's debts. Even Jim's money added to the meagre assets of Fred, Bob, Dick and the business still didn't quite produce enough to pay off all the debts. So Jim joined his ex-pals Fred, Bob and Dick in the bankruptcy court and was declared personally bankrupt.

So this is another problem with partnerships. One partner, like Jim, who happened to have more personal wealth than all the rest, could find himself in the undesirable position of being personally responsible not just for the debts of the business but also for debts run up irresponsibly by one member of that partnership. It may seem unjust, but it's the law.

This kind of threat overhanging a partnership can be a bigger handicap than all the other partnership disadvantages put together. It is for this reason that many partnerships decide to opt for a limited company as their form of business ownership.

The advantages of forming a partnership

Let's assume that having read the chapter so far, having thought about all the pros and cons of partnerships and of unlimited liability, you have decided that a partnership is the best form of business ownership for your business. In that case you should be able to fill in the section below.

List ten reasons why a joint venture with your chosen partner(s) will exploit your business idea more successfully than if you were a sole trader.

My partner(s) is suitable because:

1
2
3
4
5
6
7
8
9
10

You need to be very clear in your own mind exactly why each partner in your proposed venture is good for the business, and they must be able to fill in ten good points about you. It is a good idea not only that all members of a prospective partnership should do this exercise, but that afterwards they should sit down together and discuss the results. This would be a valuable exercise for three reasons:

1 It encourages open discussion and helps the partners to feel relaxed about expressing their opinions of each other.

2 It is good for the partnership for each partner to know that he is valued and to know why he is valued by the others.

3 It is essential that all the partners have the same idea about each others' strengths and each others' roles within the business. It's no good Fred looking forward to the start of the new business because he will be able to spend all his time designing furniture if the other partners want him mainly because they think he will be good at going out and selling it to the wholesalers and retailers.

The partnership agreement

If you are attracted to the idea of a partnership and all the partners have discussed their roles openly and are happy with their own and each others' roles, you are ready to get on with forming the partnership.

The formalities that you are legally required to conform to if you want to start trading as a partnership are few. The legal position is exactly the same as it is for the sole trader except that in the case of a partnership all the names of the owners have to be clearly shown in all the dealings of the business (see page 62 for details). However, in order to safeguard the interests of all partners and to lay a good foundation of mutual understanding which will aid the partners' long-term ability to cooperate, it is essential to start by drawing up a proper partnership agreement.

A partnership agreement is not something that need cost you a lot of money. As shown in the specimen agreement below, most of the points are issues which almost all people forming a partnership would discuss and reach an informal agreement about anyway. All you need to do is to record these points on paper.

Partnership Agreement

1 Name of the business.

2 Full name and address of each partner.

3 Nature of the business.

4 Date on which trading is to start.

5 Amount of capital to be put into the business by each partner.

6 How the profits (or losses) are to be shared between the partners.

7 The voting rights of each partner.

8 The frequency with which partnership meetings should be held.

9 The salary of each partner.

10 The role of each partner.

11 The duration of the partnership.

12 Arrangements for dissolving the partnership or releasing a partner.

13 Arbitration procedure if partners can't reach agreement.

14 Method of admitting new partners.

15 Arrangements to cover the retirement or death of a partner.

16 Arrangements concerning a partner's absence from work (for example, through sickness or accident).

17 Partners' entitlement to holidays.

18 Arrangements concerning the annual auditing of the partnership's accounts.

19 Responsibility for keeping the partnership's books and for preparing and circulating regular management accounts to keep all partners fully informed of the business's financial position.

20 Banking arrangements including arrangements for signing cheques.

21 Insurance cover to be taken out.

22 Who can sign contracts for the firm and within what limits.

The best thing at this stage is to sit down and discuss each item with your proposed partner(s) and see if you can come up with a form of words for each item that you can all agree on.

As you reach a consensus over each item, somebody should be responsible for writing down the terms that have been agreed. Make sure that all the partners are happy with the exact form of wording that has been used. When you have covered all the items get the agreement typed. You have now reached the stage where you should be prepared to pay for some professional advice to ensure that the wording and form of your agreement is correct.

Partnership insurance

We have already compared a partnership to a marriage. Most married couples feel the need for some kind of life insurance.

Partners usually have even more reason for this kind of insurance cover, but much less frequently do they take it out. Partnership insurance can be quite cheap and it can yield valuable benefits. For full details see Chapter 7.

A trial period

Traditionally, couples got engaged before they got married. Nowadays many just live together. Why? Many do it because they want to make sure that they can get on with each other day in, day out, before getting permanently attached. Sensible isn't it? So why don't partners do it? It is certainly true that most partners don't have a trial period of working together before the partnership is formed. Of course, it's often difficult to do this. There are all kinds of dilemmas during the trial period, such as: who is controlling the business, who owns products that are made or new ideas that are developed, and who is taking the risk?

These kinds of doubts often put people off the idea of a trial run, and they are certainly real problems, but they have to be compared with the potential problems of a failed partnership. If a three month trial period serves to prevent three incompatible people from forming a partnership it would have been worth all those problems. With care and a lot of discussion it would be possible in many cases to draw up a three month temporary agreement under which prospective partners cooperated on a self-employed basis. It would not be easy, but it is well worth investigating as the safest way of forming a partnership.

Limited company

A limited company is a very different kind of business ownership from the two we have looked at so far. You could say that:

A sole trader is: an **individual** who is in business to make money.

A partnership is: a **group of people** who are in business to make money.

A limited company is: an **organization** which is in business to make money.

A limited company is a legal entity, just like a person. As such it has a separate identity from the people associated with it. There may be three types of individuals connected with a limited company:

1 Shareholders: are people who own shares in the business, and are thus owners of the business.

2 Directors: are people appointed by the shareholders to run the business on their behalf and to make day-to-day decisions concerning the running of that business.

3 Employees: are people who work for the business.

The directors are often the shareholders too, especially in a small company. Employees can be shareholders and full-time directors would almost certainly be employees. The shareholders and directors could change at any time but the company continues to exist and still has the same obligations, assets and liabilities. As a separate legal entity the limited company has sole responsibility for its debts. This means that the company's shareholders (owners) do not have responsibility for those debts. The owners' liability is limited to the money that they have invested to buy shares in the company, which is where the term 'limited liability' comes from.

Forming a limited company

There are three ways of forming a limited company:

1 Do it yourself.
2 Buy a company 'off-the-shelf'.
3 Have a company 'tailor-made' by your solicitor or accountant.

1 **The 'do–it–yourself' method.** This is the cheapest way of forming a limited company. It would only cost you the £50 fee that you would have to pay to the Registrar of Companies. However, you would have quite a lot of paperwork and procedure to plough through and some fairly complex forms to fill in. It would not be an impossible task, but it would be extremely time-consuming for anybody with no prior experience of company formation. An explanatory booklet called *Notes for Guidance* is available from:

The Registrar of Companies, Companies House, Crown Way, Maindy, Cardiff CF4 3UZ. Tel: 0222 388588.

2 **An 'off-the-shelf' company.** There are a large number of company formation agents in the United Kingdom who make a living by forming companies with names that have not been used before, paying the government duty of £50 and then reselling them for around £100 to £130. These are 'off-the-shelf' companies that the agent already has in 'stock'. You can therefore have your limited company very quickly, some agencies even offering a 'same-day service'. You can find names and addresses of company agents in many places, including:

1 Business to business ads in *The Sunday Times*.
2 Business magazines like *Business Success*.

3 *Exchange and Mart,* Business Services section.
4 The Small Firms Service.

The major disadvantage of this method of company formation is that you cannot choose the name of your own company. Clearly the companies which already exist on-the-shelf already have a name. In fact, due to the shortage of more common names, many off-the-shelf companies have quite odd names. However, since the name of a company can be so important for creating the right image, you may not want a 'way-out' name. In which case you would have two alternatives:

1 You could have the name of your off-the-shelf company changed. The disadvantage is that it would take an additional four to five weeks and would cost another £50 to £80.

2 You could keep your rather unsuitable company name but use a different one as your trading name. It would be this trading name which would be recognized by the public, but you would have to follow the regulations concerning business names which are outlined on pages 61-3.

3 A 'tailor-made' company. If you have enough time and a little more money you can have a limited company tailor-made to your exact requirements. You could have this done by a company formation agency or your accountant or solicitor could perform the service for you. You should allow up to £300 and up to two months from start to finish.

How limited is limited liability?

We will now look at the three main ways in which you could incur personal liability as a director of a limited company.

Threats to limited liability include:

1 Personal guarantees.

2 National Insurance contributions.

3 The Insolvency Act, 1985.

The best way to illustrate these problems is through the imaginary case of Bill who has set up a small business.

Bill's case

Bill formed a limited company from the outset because he was not going to increase his insecurity any more than necessary. Bill formed a company called 'WJK Engineering Ltd' with 100 issued shares. Bill had 99 shares at £1 each with his wife as the other shareholder and director. At this stage his total family liability was limited to £100 and this was the way that Bill wanted to keep it.

1 Personal guarantees. Limited liability may be a very good thing for the directors of limited companies, but it is not always such a big advantage for people or organizations that the company owes money to. And they know it. Therefore a new small limited company with no track record and no reputation may find that people have a marked reluctance to allow that limited company to owe them any money. However, if a creditor has the personal guarantee of a director (or several directors) to repay any debts the chances of recovering the money are much higher because the individuals can be taken to court if necessary and their personal assets could be seized to settle any debts. Therefore, if as a director of a limited company you give a personal guarantee, you are no better off with respect to that particular debt than you would be as a sole trader.

There are four common instances where you might be asked to give personal guarantees in the early days of trading as a limited company.

a The bank. If you want to borrow money from the bank, you will almost certainly be required to give some kind of guarantee that the money will be repaid.

Bill's bank loan

> If Bill's company borrows £10,000 from the bank and Bill as a director gives a personal guarantee to repay that money, then his liability is still limited, but instead of being limited to his share capital of £100 it is now limited to £10,100 – a big jump! Bill has promised to repay that £10,000 to the bank whatever happens to WJK Engineering Ltd.

However, there are ways of borrowing money from the banks without giving personal guarantees. Here are some suggestions.

1 Banks do occasionally lend money without security if the idea is good enough and your proposition is sufficiently well presented (see Chapters 12 and 13).

2 It is quite common for banks to take out a fixed and floating charge on the assets of the company. If your company clearly has sufficient assets to cover the loan you wish to take out, the bank may be prepared to accept a fixed and floating charge instead of personal guarantees.

3 It may be that certain types of loan could limit your personal liability, for example, the government's Loan Guarantee Scheme. See Chapter 12 for more details.

b Premises. If you are leasing premises the landlord might want you to give a personal guarantee to abide by the terms of the lease.

Bill's lease

Bill needs to rent a small workshop. Let's assume that the rent is
£3000 per annum and it is available on a ten year lease. If Bill
signs the lease personally rather than on behalf of the company he
has just accepted a potential liability of £30,000. His total personal
liability has now gone up from the original £100 to £40,100!

Are there any alternatives?

1 Shopping around. In our example, Bill was rather unlucky in
choosing a landlord who was demanding such extensive personal
guarantees. Many property owners will lease premises to limited
companies without asking for any personal guarantees from
directors. It therefore pays to shop around (see Chapter 6).

2 Managed workshops. The concept of managed workshops is
explained in much more detail in Chapter 6. Suffice it to say at this
stage that there are a growing number of managed workshop type
premises which are specifically geared to meeting the needs of
small new businesses. If you want to restrict your personal liability,
these kind of premises make a lot of sense.

3 A charge on the company's assets. If it turns out to be impossible
to acquire premises without giving some kind of guarantee to the
landlord, you should investigate the possibility of limiting the extent
of the guarantee. The first step here is to see if there is any way in
which the company rather than you personally can give a
satisfactory guarantee to the landlord. It may be possible for the
company to give the landlord some kind of charge over its assets.

4 A limited personal guarantee. As a last resort you could offer a
limited personal guarantee. Using the example of Bill's workshop at
£3000 per annum rent, you could say to the landlord that you
would personally guarantee to pay any unpaid rent plus
compensation of up to one year's rent for time in which the
premises remained unoccupied. This offer should be enough to
keep all but the most avaricious landlord happy. It would give him a
whole year in which to re-let the premises, which should be more
than adequate.

c Suppliers. You might find that personal guarantees are also
demanded by suppliers of a new limited company which wants to
open a trade account. How might this affect Bill's position?

Bill's credit guarantees

Bill's new company would rely for a large proportion of its
materials on two main suppliers, one a steel stockholder and the

other a local wholesaler of general engineering supplies. A typical engineering business has quite high working capital requirements as steel and other materials have to be bought before money is received from customers for the finished job. Bill's start-up capital was not enough to cover all his working capital requirements, so he was hoping to make up the difference with credit from his two main suppliers. When Bill approached the suppliers, both were keen to do business with him and offered him all sorts of benefits including 48 hour delivery, technical back-up and an excellent range of stock. However, when it came to credit both were more cautious. They both knew how tight money was in the engineering industry and how one bad payer at the end of the line could have a knock-on effect through a number of firms. Since WJK Engineering Ltd was an unknown quantity both suppliers were reluctant to extend credit, preferring to supply on a cash on delivery basis. Bill knew he did not have the cash to purchase materials on that basis, so in order to get suppliers he offered to give personal guarantees to cover his credit from the suppliers. Bill thought that he might need up to £4000 worth of steel on credit and up to £2000 of general supplies. WJK Engineering Ltd was accordingly granted a credit limit of £4000 and £2000 respectively by the two suppliers and in both cases repayment was guaranteed by Bill.

What has this done to Bill's personal liability? He has now added a potential personal liability of £6000 to the £40,100 he has already accumulated. This means that his personal liability has now gone up from the original £100 to £46,100. It's not looking very limited any more, is it?

d Lease of equipment. Small businesses are often encouraged to lease rather than buy equipment or vehicles. This encouragement may come from books, magazines, even bank managers. However, it can be a quick way of accumulating more glossy hardware than your young business can realistically pay for, and it will almost certainly lead to an extension of your personal liability. Let's return to WJK Engineering Ltd.

Bill's new van

Before he had been in business very long, Bill realized that he could operate much more efficiently if he had a van large enough to do his own delivering to customers. He spoke to a number of reps from local commercial vehicle dealers who were quick to point out lots of other advantages! Bill would save money by not having to use carriers, he would gain customers through building a reputation for prompt and reliable delivery, a new van would improve his image and it would be a mobile advertisement for his business in the area. Bill wondered how he had ever managed without one. However, a meeting with the bank manager started off in a very disappointing way. The bank manager was very unimpressed with the whole thing, and said it would increase Bill's borrowing and his gearing. Bill thought that gearing was something to do with his van, so he nodded sagely, hoping the interview would take a turn for the better. And it did. The bank manager wondered if Bill had thought of leasing a spanking new van. Bill hadn't, nor did he know that the bank just happened to have its own leasing company which would finance the whole deal. And it did. The leasing company bought the van for £10,000 and Bill was to hire the van for 60 months. Following the final monthly instalment Bill would become the van's proud owner.

In reality Bill's new van represented a considerable liability. If he ever found it impossible to continue with the monthly repayments the leasing company would almost certainly take repossession of the van, sell it at auction and present Bill with an invoice covering his outstanding liabilities. The van could raise much less at auction than it was really worth, auctioneers fees would have to be paid, together with the leasing company's administrative charges and penalty fees. If Bill were forced to default in the first year of his leasing agreement this unquantifiable liability could amount to several thousand pounds.

2 National Insurance contributions. This is not likely to cause such a major threat to your limited liability as personal guarantees but it is a personal liability that you should be aware of. It is not uncommon for companies in financial difficulties to get behind with paying their employees' income tax and National Insurance contributions to the Inland Revenue. This money is not the firm's money. It has been deducted from employees' wages on behalf of the Inland Revenue and should be paid over every month. Moreover, if the National Insurance contributions are not paid the employees' entitlement to benefits may be jeopardized. It is for this reason that the law makes the directors of limited companies personally responsible for paying over the National Insurance contributions which have been deducted from employees' pay.

This could amount to quite a lot of money. As well as the employee's contribution there is also an employer's contribution. Directors of limited companies are personally liable for both. For a small firm with ten staff, which had fallen about three months behind, it could easily amount to about £3000.

The best advice here is to keep up-to-date with your monthly payments to the Inland Revenue. Apart from the fact that you have a moral obligation to your staff it is also in your own self-interest.

Bill's limited liability now

Although the potential personal liabilities that Bill could incur on the van leasing deal and through arrears of National Insurance contributions are not quantifiable, they could, together, quite easily amount to over £4000, thus pushing his total personal liability to over £50,000.

Such a high personal liability would almost certainly be enough to make Bill personally bankrupt if his business failed. His limited liability is therefore of no value whatsoever to him and he would have been better advised to adopt the less expensive, sole trader form of ownership.

Of course, Bill's story is wholly fictitious and rather far-fetched. It is not meant to be seen as an indictment of banks, leasing companies, landlords or any other organization to whom Bill owed money. It is meant to stress in the strongest terms the potential dangers that can lie ahead of the unwary new business owner who rushes into financial commitments. The moral of the story is that whatever form of business ownership you adopt, you should approach all long-term financial arrangement with extreme caution.

3 **The Insolvency Act, 1985.** In October 1985 the new Insolvency Act was passed by Parliament. It is designed to deter some of the more flagrant abuses of the limited liability system, for example, people clearly defrauding customers and/or suppliers, going into voluntary liquidation and then setting up again straight away doing exactly the same thing. Most people would support the Act in this objective, but in attempting to stamp out the abuses of limited liability by the unprincipled few it will probably have the effect of reducing the value of limited liability for the majority of decent businessmen.

There are a number of important new measures introduced by the Insolvency Act which have altered the position of limited companies and their directors.

a *Wrongful trading.* A new offence called 'wrongful trading' has been created by the Insolvency Act. It means that forming a limited company no longer guarantees owner–directors the protection of limited liability. Under the new Insolvency Act directors can be made personally liable for debts incurred by the company if 'the director knew or ought to have concluded that there was no reasonable prospect that the company would avoid going into insolvent liquidation and thereafter failed to take every step to minimize the loss to the company's creditors'.

b Disqualification of unfit directors. Any director found guilty of wrongful trading is now in danger of being judged unfit to be involved in the management of a company and would therefore be liable to disqualification for a minimum period of two years.

c Restrictions on company names. In order to curb the practice of companies going into liquidation and resuming trading almost straight away with a very similar name, it will now be illegal for a director of a company which has gone into insolvent liquidation to be involved in any other company using the same or a similar name within five years of the failure of the original company.

d Administrators. A new office of administrator or administrative receiver has been created. Administrators are people who can step into and take charge of companies that are in danger of going into liquidation. An administrator can be called in by the shareholders, directors or creditors of a company in difficulties. The administrator would manage the company's affairs in the best interests of the creditors. He might cease operations straight away and sell everything off as quickly as possible, he might try to sell the company or parts of it as a going concern or he might conclude that the whole operation could be made profitable if better managed. Whatever the case, his objective would be to ensure that in the long run the creditors received as much of their money as possible from the company. The administrator would be in complete charge of the company. He could dismiss directors and take any actions that he considered to be in the best interests of the creditors.

It will be through contacting the administrator very early, as soon as the company is experiencing difficulties, that directors will most surely avoid the charge of wrongful trading. However, this is almost bound to cause problems as most company directors are in that position because they value their independence and like to remain in control of their own destiny. Many directors will feel that they stand more chance of saving their company if they retain full control. If they fail, they may then be faced with the charge of wrongful trading with the possibility of being made personally liable for some of the company's debts.

Limited liability – a summary

There is no doubt that limited liability does increase your security. It means that, apart from National Insurance contributions, you cannot be held personally responsible for debts incurred by the business unless you sign an agreement offering a personal guarantee or a charge over your personal assets, and provided you do not contravene the provisions of the Insolvency Act. It also offers a formal arrangement for the ownership of the company which may be beneficial to those considering a partnership.

On the other hand, forming a limited company should not be seen as a way of guaranteeing your personal security, whatever happens to the business. No responsible organization will lend money or extend credit to a limited company whose ability to repay is in doubt. In such situations you would therefore be required to furnish some kind of personal guarantee. Other disadvantages of limited companies which apply to most new businesses include higher formation costs, and higher overheads for professional services such as accountancy and tax disadvantages. However, you should seek professional guidance about the relevance of these points to your own particular circumstances, as explained in Chapter 4.

Workers' cooperative

What is a workers' cooperative?

An alternative and increasingly popular form of business ownership is the workers' cooperative. There is no single legal definition of a workers' cooperative and the exact rules governing different cooperatives can vary. However, the following guidelines would be accurate in most cases:

1 The business is owned and controlled by the people who work in it on the basis of one person one vote.

2 Only people employed in the business have a right to be members.

3 All the people employed in the business have a right to be members.

4 Capital employed by the business is taken in the form of loans, not shares and therefore carries no element of control.

A cooperative does not have to be a socialist type commune where everybody is paid the same wages, jobs are rotated and every decision is subject to a cumbersome democratic process. They are not usually companies without managers and may not even operate a profit-sharing scheme. However, most people have certain idealistic motives for deciding that a cooperative is the right kind of business ownership for them, and most cooperatives, in spirit as well as in letter, are genuinely controlled by all the people who work in it, though they may perform a wide variety of different jobs within the company. Many of the supporters of the workers' cooperative movement would argue that common ownership is all about improving the quality of working life.

Are there many workers' cooperatives?

Workers' cooperatives are being formed at the rate of roughly one per day at the present time. Most are very small but some employ hundreds of people. Cooperatives are involved in a wide variety of sectors including chemicals, building, textiles, publishing, catering, wholefoods and many more. Contrary to popular belief, workers' cooperatives have a good track record. Statistics show that if success is measured in terms of surviving for at least four years, workers' cooperatives have had a better track record over the last decade than all other forms of new business. Maybe this is accounted for by the considerable network of advice and support agencies that exist to help new workers' cooperatives.

How do you form a workers' cooperative?

Forming a workers' cooperative is a very complex subject and one which is beyond the scope of this book. It is necessary to seek qualified help on the legal form of the common ownership agreement and expert counselling on the inter-personal aspects of forming and running a cooperative. Therefore, the remainder of this section will do no more than point readers who are interested in the idea of workers' cooperatives in the direction of suitably sound advice. As already indicated, there is no shortage of valuable help, including the following organizations:

The National Cooperative Development Agency, 20 Albert Embankment, London SE1. Tel: 01 211 7033.

Established by the government in 1978 to promote all forms of cooperation, it now has many local branches where advice and practical help will be available. Contact head office to find the whereabouts of your closest Cooperative Development Agency.

The Industrial Common Ownership Movement Ltd, The Corn Exchange, Leeds LS8 2LQ. Tel: 0532 720205.

A long-standing organization offering a variety of services to common ownerships including advice and training. It provides a very good set of model rules for cooperatives and help with registering. It has also established a funding organization to lend money to cooperatives:

Industrial Common Ownership Finance Ltd, 1 St. Giles St, Northampton NN1 1SA. Tel: 0604 37563.

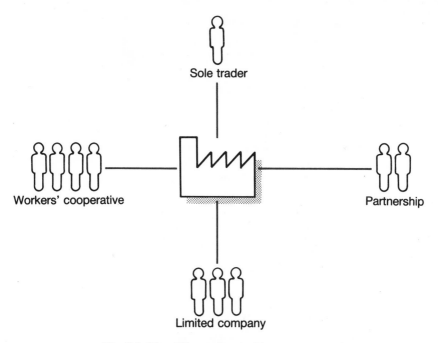

Fig. 3.1 The different forms of business ownership

Franchises

A franchise is a way of buying a ready made business package rather than starting your own business from scratch. You would buy a franchise from a franchisor, who is a person or a company with a good business idea which they are prepared to sell to a franchisee. The franchise is the agreement they both sign which governs the sale of the business idea.

Franchising has been very common in the USA for many years and is now rapidly growing in popularity on this side of the Atlantic. There are more franchises around than most people realize. Many fast food outlets are run on a franchise basis including Spud-U-Like and Wimpy. Retailing is another popular area of franchising. The Benetton fashion stores, the Phildar wool shops and the Holland and Barratt health foods shops are all examples of franchises. Service businesses are particularly easy to franchise, and are often amongst the cheapest franchises to buy. Well known names include Prontaprint, Mobiletune, Dyno-Rod, Appollo Window Blinds and Budget Rent-a-Car. Each outlet of all these different businesses is owned by a different person who runs it as his own small business.

The advantages of franchising

1 Advice from the franchisor about setting up your business properly. This could include help with:

   a choice of location
   b suitability of premises
   c refurbishing of premises
   d financial planning
   e raising finance
   f legal formalities like company formation, partnership agreement, property lease, etc
   g insurance requirements
   h employing staff
   i marketing

2 A business name which is already well known, like Holland and Barratt or Benetton is a very valuable asset.

3 National advertising of the whole group may be carried out by the franchisor in return for contributions from franchisees.

4 Supplies of materials or stock, possibly at advantageous prices as a result of group buying power.

5 A tried and tested business idea with a proven market demand which is already working well in other places, thus reducing the risks normally associated with starting a new small business.

6 The all important trade knowledge which was stressed so much in Chapter 2 will be provided by the franchisor, so you do have the opportunity of moving into a new trade which you have had no previous experience of.

The disadvantages of franchising

1 **The cost.** This can be a very big disadvantage. You need to have a lot of capital if you are going to invest in most franchises. Some franchises which need a lot of equipment and expensive town centre premises require a six figure investment. A more common figure would be anywhere from £25,000 to £75,000. This would include most of the retailing franchises. This would cover your total starting up costs including equipment, fixtures and fittings, initial stock and any fee payable to the franchisor. Some of the service franchises which need a fairly low investment for premises, stock and equipment are available for below £10,000 but very few good franchises cost as little as £5000.

There are three main aspects to the cost of a franchise:

a Start-up costs. Your initial investment in the business will be decided for you by the franchisor, so it is not usually possible to save money here. Most franchisors lay down exact requirements partly because they say they know what kind of investment is most successful but mainly because they want to protect the image of the operation.

b A lump sum franchise fee. Most franchises involve the payment of a lump sum fee to cover the right to use the business name, trademarks, methods, etc, and as payment for the initial advice package. This sum can amount to thousands of pounds, so you really do need to be certain that you are getting value for money.

c Royalties. In most franchise agreements, payments to the franchisor do not end with the initial lump sum payment. The way in which the franchisor really makes it worth his while to licence his business idea in this way is by making franchisees pay ongoing royalties. Every year you would have to pay a certain percentage of your turnover to the franchisor. You may get certain benefits in return such as ongoing advice and national advertising of the organization, but many franchise operations will charge you an extra fee above the royalty for any national advertising. Royalties could be 5 to 10 per cent of turnover in lower profit margin operations but can be as much as 40 per cent of turnover in some of the service industry franchises. Giving up a percentage of your turnover in this way *ad infinitum* is something that some people may find very hard to accept.

2 Lack of independence. If you buy a franchise you do own your own business but you would not be as independent as somebody who started their own business from scratch. Apart from paying royalties every year, the franchise agreement may place many restrictions on the way that you can run your business, because the franchisor wants to ensure that all the outlets retain the same corporate image. In the long run you may find this irritating, and restrictive.

3 Supplies. When you first start your business it can be an advantage to be able to get your supplies through the franchising organization. Getting suitable supplies at reasonable prices can often be a difficult task for new businesses, especially if they want them on credit. However, as time goes on all businesses develop a lot more contact with suppliers and learn how to negotiate much more attractive prices. If a franchise agreement tied you down to having all your supplies or even a certain percentage from the franchisor, you might find this very restrictive. You might want to buy different goods, or you might be able to buy alternative goods more cheaply elsewhere.

4 'Shady' franchise deals. There is a world of difference between a good franchise and a bad franchise. The whole concept of franchising earned itself a very bad name in the 1970s because there were a significant number of franchises that were not worth the paper that the agreement was written on. Things have improved since then, but it is important to distinguish between good and bad franchise deals.

Evaluating franchise opportunities

If you are seriously interested in a franchise then the most important task that you have to perform is the evaluation of the franchisor and the franchise package. To go into this properly is beyond the scope of this book and is not a job for the new businessman to perform without expert advice. You should therefore consider using the following sources of expert advice before reaching any kind of agreement over a franchise.

1 Reading. You should aim to make yourself thoroughly conversant with franchising so that you can form your own initial opinions of franchise packages before you consult the professional experts. There are two books which are highly recommended in this respect:

Taking up a Franchise, G. Golzen, C. Barrow and J. Severn, Kogan Page Ltd, 1988.

This is a well known book which you could order from your local bookshop or through the library.

How to Evaluate a Franchise, M. Mendelsohn, Franchise Publications.

Available from: *Franchise Publications, James House, 37 Nottingham Rd, London SW17 7EA. Tel: 01 767 1371.*

There are also some magazines which provide useful up-to-date information about franchising including case studies of businesses which are run as franchises. They will also contain lists of franchise opportunities with details of fees, royalties and investment costs. Two publications are particularly useful here:

Business Success, already referred to in Chapter 2, is a monthly magazine costing £1.75 per copy, available from most large newsagents.

Franchise World, devoted entirely to franchising and published once every three months by Franchise Publications (address above).

2 The British Franchise Association. This is a trade organization made up of most of the leading franchisors whose object is to promote 'ethical franchising'. It requires its members to adhere to a code of conduct which protects the interests of franchisees. If you are interested in a specific franchise it is a big help if the franchisor is a member of the BFA, because although it won't guarantee the success of a franchise it does give you confidence that if you do have any problems you can appeal to the BFA who would investigate the matter. You can contact the British Franchise Association at:

15 The Poynings, Iver SL0 9DA. Tel: 0753 653546.

3 **The bank manager.** Once you have a clear idea about the franchise that interests you the bank can be very useful in helping you to evaluate it. Most banks look favourably on franchising as a less risky way of starting in business, provided you have the necessary capital and provided that you are buying a good franchise. Your bank manager is therefore likely to be a very useful adviser at this stage.

4 **Your solicitor.** You must consult a solicitor before you sign a franchise agreement. However good and safe the agreement appears to be it would be incredibly risky to go ahead and sign it without proper legal advice. Do make sure that the solicitor you use has specialist knowledge of franchising.

Business names

Do you have to register your business name?

The answer is no! Before 1982 you had to pay £1 to register your name with the Registry of Business Names in London but since then the Registry has been closed and there has been no legal obligation to register a business name. If you form a limited company your business name along with all the other details of your company is recorded at Companies House. If, however, you are a sole trader or a partnership you no longer have to register your business. You do have to conform to certain requirements though, and these are laid down in the Business Names Act of 1985.

The Business Names Act, 1985

The regulations contained in the Business Names Act cover all businesses which trade under a name that is different from the name(s) of the owner(s) of the business. If John Smith is a plumber and he trades as John Smith, J. Smith or J. Smith, Plumber, then this is fine, but if he trades as Kwikplum, Fixaleak, or any name other than his own he must conform to the requirements of the Business Names Act. The Act would also apply to limited companies which do not trade under the name of the limited company but use a different trading name.

A business using a trade name must conform to three basic

requirements. These can be called the 'three Ds': *Documents, Disclosure, Display.*

Documents. The name(s) of all the owners of the business must be displayed on all business documents. An address in the UK must also be shown. Included among such documents would be letter-heading, order forms and invoices.

Disclosure. You must disclose information concerning the ownership of the business, in writing, immediately that you are asked for it by anybody who has dealings with the business. If this situation arose you would probably hand them a sheet of the firm's letter-heading.

Blue Ball Gowns Ltd

Particulars of ownership as required by the Business Names Act of 1985

Names of proprietors:

James Alan Henderson
Rosemary Henderson
William Richards
Sheila Ann Roberts

Address of business:

23 London Road
Smalltown
Wessex
SM1 2YZ

Fig. 3.2 Example of notice showing ownership of business

Display. A notice concerning the ownership of the business must be prominently displayed in a part of the business premises to which customers and suppliers have regular access. It should say something along the lines shown by the example opposite.

NB The names should be the full names of the owners, not forgetting that the owner could be a limited company rather than an individual. The address must be an address in Britain at which documents can be served on the business. This official address does not have to be the your main place of business. It could be an accommodation address or your accountant's office (with his permission). It does not matter as long as it is in the UK and it is an address through which contact with the business can be guaranteed.

Restrictions on business names

You can't just call your business anything. In particular, names which appear to give your business a status, or endorsement which it doesn't have are not allowed. John Smith can't call his business Royal Plumbing Repairs. There are other words which imply government patronage which can only be used with the permission of the Secretary of State for Trade. These include, 'National', 'International', 'European', 'British', 'Authority', 'Board', 'Council', 'Association', 'Assurance', 'Society'. Some names might require the permission of the relevant professional body, for example the use of the word 'Apothecary' in your business name would need the consent of The Pharmaceutical Society of Great Britain.

It is obviously not permissible to use the word 'Ltd' unless your business is registered as a limited company.

Despite all these regulations it is possible, and it does happen, that two businesses could end up with the same trading name. Very often, the wealthier of the two will buy the name from the other, but if neither side will give way and a battle develops, the business which could prove first use of the name would have priority.

Summary

1 The sole trader is the least costly and simplest form of business ownership. It does however rely on the owner having sufficient capital and appropriate expertise, some may find it arduous and lonely and most sole traders are vulnerable at times of ill health.

2 Partnerships retain the financial advantages of the sole trader and can benefit from the additional capital, expertise and support brought by partners. The main disadvantages revolve around potential disagreements between the partners and great care needs to be taken to minimize this risk.

3 Both sole traders and partnerships suffer from the problem of unlimited liability.

4 Limited companies are more costly in terms of taxation, formation costs and accountancy fees. They can offer additional security for partnerships; and the state benefits available to employees (but not necessarily to the self-employed) and the status of a limited company can be advantageous.

5 Personal liability cannot be avoided simply by forming a company. The Insolvency Act is designed to prevent the unscrupulous from sheltering behind limited liability but even the most honest and cautious business may be caught out by personal guarantees and all company directors are personally liable for the unpaid National Insurance contributions of their employees.

6 Workers' cooperatives offer an interesting though complex alternative form of business ownership and have a relatively good track record.

7 Good franchises probably offer the least risky way of starting a business but they often require high start-up capital and need to be evaluated very carefully beforehand.

8 Sole traders and partnerships are under no legal obligation to register their business name but there are constraints on the type of name which may be used and regulations concerning the display and disclosure of the names of the owners of the business.

4 Using the experts

Aims of this chapter

To examine:

- The areas where professional advice is most important
- The extent to which you should make use of professional advisers (given that they are usually expensive)
- How the new business owner should go about the process of choosing professional advisers
- When this should be done

These will be discussed within the context of the three main professional advisers that almost all new businesses will need:

1 An accountant.
2 A solicitor.
3 A bank manager.

Choosing an accountant

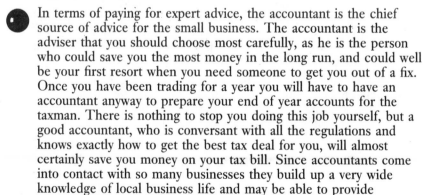

In terms of paying for expert advice, the accountant is the chief source of advice for the small business. The accountant is the adviser that you should choose most carefully, as he is the person who could save you the most money in the long run, and could well be your first resort when you need someone to get you out of a fix. Once you have been trading for a year you will have to have an accountant anyway to prepare your end of year accounts for the taxman. There is nothing to stop you doing this job yourself, but a good accountant, who is conversant with all the regulations and knows exactly how to get the best tax deal for you, will almost certainly save you money on your tax bill. Since accountants come into contact with so many businesses they build up a very wide knowledge of local business life and may be able to provide valuable advice in the following areas:

a choosing your bank manager and other advisers
b partnership or company formation
c financial planning
d raising finance
e local property values
f general business advice

There can be a world of difference between a good and bad accountant. A bad accountant will look after your annual accounts and tax affairs, but he will do little else, apart from charge you a lot of money! You need an accountant who:

1 Will take a real interest in the success of your business.
2 Has a good knowledge of your kind of business.
3 Will give you a reasonable estimation of his charges.

You can satisfy yourself on these three criteria only by visiting and speaking to a number of accountants and then selecting the one who you feel is most appropriate to the needs of your business. How do you decide which accountants to go and see?

1 **Personal recommendation.** This is by far the best kind of introduction. You should consult local people in business whose judgement you trust.

2 **Other recommendations.** Agencies like the Small Firms Service and the Rural Development Commission should be able to recommend the names of accountants, as should your personal bank manager.

3 **Advertisements.** This method is not anything like as good as the personal recommendation, but advertisements do provide more general information, for instance, the sort of services offered, whether the practice specialises in a particular area, and so on.

4 *Yellow Pages.* If all else fails you will find a list of all the accountants in your area in the *Yellow Pages*, but this will only be a list of names. It would be sensible at first to ring a few up to find out whether they would be interested in taking on new small business clients.

You should resolve to visit at least three accountants for a short chat to see if you would both be happy with each other. You should not be asked to pay for this initial consultation, as no specific service will actually be provided for you.

Meeting the accountant

The main point to remember is that you should go in confidently and prepare to speak to the accountant as an equal. You are doing him a favour if you agree to let him look after your affairs. You will be paying money to him. Unless you can deal with your accountant on a one-to-one basis, you will not gain the maximum advantage from the relationship.

You would probably find it very useful to prepare a list of questions beforehand to ensure that you cover all the points that you want to know about. Take it in with you and refer to it. The accountant will think all the more of you for being methodical, and it is all too easy to forget things during the course of a brief meeting.

1 Fees. Many accountants will tell you that they can't be specific about fees because they charge on the basis of how long things take, and how much you use them. You should press them to give you an estimate. They know roughly how much their annual bill to a business the size of yours normally comes to. You also need to know what the estimate covers because some services that you may require (helping you to prepare a proposal for a bank loan, for example) would probably cost extra.

2 Qualifications. You need to ensure that the accountant is actually a qualified accountant – not all of them are! An accountant is qualified if he has any of the following letters after his name:

Chartered Accountants: ACA, FCA.

Certified Accountants: ACCA, FCCA.

If you want to make sure of an accountant's qualifications you can do so by checking up with the relevant professional body:

The Institute of Chartered Accountants, PO Box 433, Chartered Accountants Hall, Moorgate Place, London EC2P 2BJ. Tel: 01 628 7060.

The Association of Certified Accountants, 29 Lincoln's Inn Fields, London EC2A 3EE. Tel: 01 242 6855.

Members of either of these organizations are equally capable of looking after your tax affairs.

3 Specialist knowledge. How much the accountant knows about your particular kind of business. If it is something very unusual you can't expect him to know anything about it, but if it is something quite common, like a small engineering business, then you should be able to find an accountant with a reasonable knowledge of this kind of enterprise.

4 Clients. You should ask the accountant to give you the names of some of his clients so that you can approach them to ask their opinion of him. This would be especially useful if some of these clients were in a similar line of business to yours. You do need to be realistic, however, because he is not likely to give you the names of clients unless he has good relations with them.

5 Computers. You may be planning to computerize your accounts in the foreseeable future. If so, you need an accountant with a sound knowledge of computers who could give you good advice.

6 Aid for small businesses. Any professional adviser to a small business is not worth having these days unless he has an excellent knowledge of all the various schemes of assistance available to the small business. An accountants job is to save you money, and making maximum use of any government aid is vital for any new business trying to establish itself.

7 Your accountant. Don't take it for granted that the accountant you are talking to will be the one who always deals with your affairs. Your initial contact may well be with the senior partner, but it could be the unqualified junior who gets to handle your work. Also, what if your accountant is on holiday or off sick and you need to see someone in a hurry? If it is a small practice, would there be another qualified accountant for you to see?

8 Your business. Does the accountant seem to be taking a genuine interest in you, in your plans and in your business? If he doesn't at this stage there's not much hope that he will later on.

 9 Chemistry. Did you like him? Do you think you could get on with him, confide in him, trust him? This personal chemistry is probably more important than anything else in the long run. Do not choose an accountant with whom you don't feel at ease.

What about a solicitor?

You may need a solicitor for one of the following purposes:

1 Forming a company. Although, as indicated in Chapter 3, you may simply use a company formation agent or your accountant for this purpose.

2 Drawing up a partnership agreement. Chapter 3 recommended that a professional adviser be used to check any agreement between partners, but your accountant may be more appropriate if he has closely followed your business activities from the beginning.

3 Franchise or workers' cooperative. Due to the more complex nature of agreements for such businesses a solicitor would almost certainly be required.

4 Premises. Your local solicitor is likely to be at his best when dealing with property matters rather than business matters. Any purchase of premises and most leases would require the involvement of a solicitor. Some rented premises (for example, managed workshop schemes) may have such simple agreements that a solicitor is not necessary. Even so, it would be worth checking with your accountant or an organization like the Small Firms Service that it is as straightforward as it appears.

5 Special agreements. You may be starting your business on the strength of a large contract with a particular customer or you may have a licensing agreement which allows you to manufacture another company's product or design. Such agreements need to be checked by a specialist commercial solicitor which may mean paying more and using a large practice in your nearest city.

If you do need to use a solicitor when you are starting your business your choice would rather depend on the nature of the work that you required him to perform. If you are using him for basic property matters your local solicitor will be ideal. If you do not already have a personal solicitor consult your accountant over a suitable choice. Your accountant should also be able to recommend a good commercial practice if necessary. Since you are basically employing a solicitor to perform a specific task on your behalf rather than to be a permanent business adviser, the choice of solicitor at this stage in your business career is much less important than your choice of accountant. However, contract law is very complex and many problems arise because small firms are tempted to cut corners in the hope of saving money on legal fees. If in doubt consult a solicitor.

The bank manager

In the long run your bank manager may give you help in any of the following ways:

1 Taking out a bank loan.
2 Arranging overdraft facilities.
3 Help with exporting, from financial help to help with finding markets or understanding the required documentation.
4 Insurance.
5 Examining a franchise agreement.
6 Leasing equipment or vehicles.
7 General business advice.

There are many ways in which a bank manager can be very valuable to a business, but the better he knows you and your business, the more likely he is to be more helpful. It is therefore a great advantage to have a bank manager who has known your business from day one and feels that he has been involved in its growth. The importance of this long term relationship is shown by the fact that many businesses follow their bank manager to another branch if he moves on, even if it is much less convenient to have their account at a bank some miles away.

Choosing your bank

All the banks offer similar services and all will be keen to have a new business account. The charges, expertise, opening hours and facilities of the different banks in your area will all be very much alike. The main difference between the banks will be in the personalities of their respective managers.

Choosing your bank manager

1 **Making the approach.** There may well only be about four or five banks to choose from in your local town so it's not a difficult job to go and see all the bank managers. Before you do that you should make as many enquiries as you can about the different managers. The opinions of other people in business are the most relevant. How do they get on with their bank manager? How helpful is he? How approachable is he? Your accountant's opinion is very important because if he has a particularly good relationship with one of the bank managers, that could prove very useful to you if you ever needed some help.

It would be worth finding out if the bank manager seems to have any particular interest in, or knowledge of, your kind of business. For example, if you were opening a sports shop and you found a bank manager whose hobby was running this would be a real bonus. It would give him a natural interest in your business and, as a result, he may give you more attention than most other businesses of your size.

It is necessary to stress two further points about approaching banks:

1 Don't pay any special attention to the bank where you have your personal account. You may have been a model customer there for years but that may count for little since it does not necessarily mean that you will be any good at running a business.

2 The initial interview with the banks is not the time to start discussing bank loans. If the subject is raised you should discuss bank loans in general terms, but stress that you have not yet completed your business plan and cannot therefore be specific about your likely requirements.

2 **Making the choice.** Choosing your bank manager is not the same as choosing your accountant. He will not be your primary source of expert business advice but he will be a very useful source of such advice. You should use him as much as possible because you will not be charged for consulting him. However, there is a

limit to how much you can realistically take advantage of him. So, unlike the process of choosing your accountant you are not really trying to convince yourself that the bank manager is good at his job. What you really want in a bank manager is somebody who you feel you can build up a good relationship with so that you stand a good chance of being able to count on his support during the lean times.

There are therefore two main criteria on which to make your choice:

1 Did you feel at ease when you were talking to him? Unless you feel that you can talk to and confide in your bank manager, you will always try to avoid going to see him. If things are bad you will try to put it off in the hope that they improve. By the time you force yourself to go and see him it may be too late. Even if things are going well, it is very useful if you can arrange to discuss your plans periodically with the bank manager. It doesn't matter if they are not yet firm plans. He may have some useful advice, ideas or even contacts to contribute.

2 Was he interested? If you were lucky enough to find a bank manager who was personally interested in the product you were going to make or sell, it would be a real bonus and a very strong reason for using that bank. You can also try to gauge the level of genuine interest that the bank manager had in your ideas.

Fig. 4.1 Banking advice for the small business

Summary

1 It takes a considerable amount of time to select the most suitable advisers. Once you have started trading you will not have the time to choose them as carefully as you should so it is important to tackle the problem as early as possible in the planning stage of your business.

2 Making this early choice is also important so that you can make use of relevant professional advice during the planning stage.

3 Your accountant will almost certainly be the most important choice of professional adviser so you should be prepared to take a great deal of time and care over your choice.

4 Your choice of accountant will be based on several factors including your perception of his professional competence, his level of interest in your plans and how well you think you could get on with him.

5 Not all new businesses will need a solicitor at the outset unless complicated legal documents such as leases or commercial agreements need to be checked. Your accountant's recommendation is probably the best way to choose a solicitor.

6 Your bank and its manager can be extremely useful to your business in the future and should therefore be chosen with great care.

7 All local banks should be visited but your choice of bank manager should be the one with whom you feel you can develop the best personal relationship.

5 Sources of help

Aims of this chapter

Many people claim to be baffled by the large and complex array of grants and other forms of assistance available to small businesses. The main aim of this chapter is therefore to give a brief and clear outline of the main sources of help for new businesses. We will also examine how useful each type of assistance is likely to be for the average new business.

The Enterprise Allowance Scheme

Under this scheme you can receive £40 per week for your first year in business. This is a most valuable subsidy because it enables you to take less capital out of the business during those critical first few months when the business will need all the working capital it can lay its hands on. The other good thing about the Enterprise Allowance Scheme is that it is easy to apply for. There are no long-winded forms to fill in and no time-consuming procedures to follow. You simply go to your local Jobcentre and ask for details. There is a simple form to fill in but the Jobcentre staff should help you to do that on the spot.

There are a number of criteria that you must satisfy if you are to receive the allowance:

1 You must have been unemployed for at least eight weeks.

2 You must be over 18 years of age.

 3 You must apply **before** you start your business.

4 You must be planning to work full-time in your business. You must also allow the Department of Employment to inspect your business at any time while you are receiving the allowance so that they can make sure that you are actually running a full-time business.

5 It is compulsory to attend a one day training session. The session explains all about the Enterprise Allowance Scheme and covers a few brief points about what it's like to run your own business. It is designed to make people aware of what they are letting themselves in for. It is not an attempt to judge your suitability for the scheme.

6 The trickiest requirement, particularly for some unemployed

people, is the necessity for the applicant to have £1000 available to invest in the business. Some businesses will have higher start-up costs than that, others can be started quite realistically with much less capital. The reason given by the Department of Employment for this requirement is that the £1000 is a sign of the serious intent of the applicant.

If you are unlikely to have this sort of money there may be a solution open to you in that the £1000 only has to be 'available' for investment in the business. Therefore if you can beg, borrow (but preferably not steal!) £1000 and have it 'available' (a bank statement or a building society book in the name of your proposed business would confirm this), you will qualify for the Enterprise Allowance Scheme. You do not have to spend it. And if your bank considers your scheme to be a good one, it may well be prepared to loan the £1000 (see Chapter 12 for further details).

Help for the unemployed

If you are unemployed but you don't find the Enterprise Allowance Scheme suited to your needs, there are a number of things you could consider if you want to start your own business. You can obviously do all your own planning, get everything ready for the start of your business, and attend any useful training courses while you are drawing benefit, but you can actually go further than this and actually start your business in a limited way without falling foul of the authorities. The following section consists of three suggestions that you might find useful:

Trading on the 'dole'

1 **Testing out your business idea.** It is possible to start trading to test out your business idea while you are still drawing supplementary benefit. You would have to tell the DSS what you were doing and you would have to declare your net earnings from self-employment. The regulations allow you to earn a small amount of money (only a few pounds per week) on top of your supplementary benefit. The key phrase here is 'net earnings', which is defined as 'income less expenses'. In the early days of running a business your expenses can quite legitimately exceed your earnings. If any net losses from one week were carried forward to the next you may be able to spend some time setting up and establishing your business without losing the right to receive your benefit payments. If you are married with children and have rent to pay, this method of starting your business could be more suitable than

the Enterprise Allowance Scheme, but you should check all the details with your local DSS office beforehand.

2 Tools and equipment. If you are drawing supplementary benefit you may even be able to get help with your start-up costs. If you can convince the DSS that helping to set you up in self-employment would eventually result in your removal from their books, they may help you! They are allowed to give out small loans towards the cost of tools and equipment in such cases.

3 Unemployment benefit. The regulations for people drawing unemployment benefit rather than supplementary benefit are different. They are also very complex. In principle you lose your right to unemployment benefit for any days on which you are unavailable for work. This means that if you were working full-time on your new business you would not be available for other work and therefore you would get not benefit – even if you were not earning anything from your business. Similarly, if you make yourself unavailable for work for only part of the week, you would lose a corresponding proportion of your benefit. Under these circumstances the Enterprise Allowance Scheme is clearly preferable. However, the Department of Employment does not make rules for Sundays, because you don't have to be available for work on Sundays. Therefore, whatever business you do on a Sunday does not affect your benefit.

Help for training and consultancy

The two main sources of help are the Training Agency and the Department of Trade and Industry.

The Training Agency

The Training Agency, formerly known as the Manpower Services Commission, is primarily involved in training people for work, and they attach great importance to training people to run their own businesses. Training Agency schemes have changed considerably over the last few years, so it is always wise to check the exact nature of current schemes, but at the time of going to press assistance was available from the Training Agency for small businesses under the title of Business Growth Training. The scheme is divided into five parts which, between them, are designed to assist a wide range of businesses, from small to large and from well established firms to prospective new ventures. It is the first two of these five options which are suitable for new businesses.

Help is also available under three other schemes:

1 Business Growth Training. Option 1: *'Your Business Success'* *kits* offers you a specially designed self-help training kit covering financial planning and the writing of a business plan. The kits are free from authorized agents appointed by the Training Agency in your area. The agents are usually business and training specialists who will also provide consultancy help.

Option 2: *Business Skills for Owner-managers* offers training courses in business skills. There are two branches to this option which may interest prospective new business owners:

a The Private Enterprise Programme is a series of thirteen one day seminars on business management skills for small firms. The topics covered are: Marketing, Selling, Sales Promotion, Finding New Products, Sources of Finance, Book-keeping, Basic Accounting, Financial Control, Managing Growth, Computers in Business, Computerized Accounting, Employing People, and Taxation.

The seminars are run on a local basis on behalf of the Training Agency by organizations such as colleges, chambers of commerce and private consultancy companies. They are heavily subsidized, and are free to firms in their first year of trading but cost £35 per seminar to other firms.

b Firmstart is aimed at businesses which have recently started trading but which are considered to have the potential for strong growth. This is defined as being able to employ ten people within the first year of trading. Firmstart is run for the Training Agency by the major business schools, and, for firms in leisure industries, by the Hotel and Catering Industry Training Board. There is a fee of £250 for the course. The Firmstart programme is spread over a period of 13 to 26 weeks and will be tailored to your individual needs. It could include the researching of your business idea, the development of a business plan, and help with the marketing of your new product or service. Tuition is provided during evenings and weekends so that the course does not interfere with your running of your business.

2 The Graduate Enterprise Programme. Designed for graduates who want to start their own business, this programme is spread over a thirteen week period during which time the prospective business owner will be assimilating the information and advice that will help him to start his new business. Course members receive an allowance of about £42 per week (though this can vary according to individual circumstances) for the duration of the programme. At intervals throughout the programme there are four separate weeks of full-time, residential courses in 'business skills'. The courses are held at some of the country's main business schools, and accommodation is provided. There is no fee for attending the Graduate Enterprise Programme.

3 Business Skills Training. Aimed at people who are thinking of starting a business, this programme consists of seven days of practical training spread over a five week period. It is free of charge. Training is provided by a range of agents, and the scheme should be available to you locally. Officially, this scheme is part of the Training Agency's Employment Training programme, but there is provision for people who are not registered unemployed to take advantage of the scheme.

Details of all these schemes are available from the Training Agency, which has a large number of local offices (addresses on pages 78-80), and a free telephone number: *0800 300 787*, on which you can request booklets about Business Growth Training.

The Department of Trade and Industry (DTI)

Help from the DTI takes the form of the Enterprise Initiative programme. As far as new businesses are concerned the most relevant part of this programme is the consultancy initiative, under which the DTI will cover half the cost (two thirds in some assisted areas) of a professional consultancy project into any of the following areas of business management: Marketing, Exporting, Business Planning, Financial and Information Systems, Quality Assurance, Design, and Manufacturing Systems.

However, with average consultancy fees of around £300 per day and projects lasting from 5 to 15 days, the total cost of a 15 day subsidized project would be £2250 (or £1500 in an assisted area). Thus, unless you have plenty of funding for your new business, you may find one of the Training Agency schemes, such as Firmstart or Business Skills Training, more suited to your needs.

If you need to find out more about DTI schemes you can ask for the *DTI Guide for Business* which outlines a large number of schemes, although many of them are suited to the needs of established businesses rather than new ones. The DTI has a telephone number for people requesting booklets on the Enterprise Initiative: *0800 500 200*, and also a general enquiries telephone number: *01 215 5000*. You can find the address and telephone number of your nearest regional office in fig. 5.2.

Fig. 5.1 Training Agency area offices

LONDON REGION

Inner London North	1st Floor 236 Grays Inn Road London WC1X 8HL	01-837 3311
Inner London South	200 Great Dover Street London SE1 4YB	01-357 7110
London East	3rd Floor Cityside House 40 Adler Street London E1 1EW	01-377 1866
London North	6th Floor 19-29 Woburn Place London WC1 0LU	01-837 1288
London South	Skyline House 200 Union Street London SE1 0LX	01-928 0800
London West	Lyric House 149 Hammersmith Road Hammersmith London W14 0QL	01-602 7227

EAST MIDLANDS & EASTERN REGION

Bedfordshire & Cambridgeshire	1st & 2nd Floors, Wesley House 19 Chapel Street Luton LU1 2SE	0582 412828
Derbyshire	4th Floor St Peter's House Gower Street Derby DE1 1SB	0332 290550
Leicestershire & Northamptonshire	1st Floor Rutland Centre Halford Street Leicester LE1 1TQ	0533 538616
Lincolnshire	5th Floor Wigford House Brayford Wharf Lincoln LN5 7AY	0522 32266
Norfolk & Suffolk	Crown House Crown Street Ipswich IP1 3HS	0473 218951
Nottinghamshire	4th Floor Lambert House Talbot Street Nottingham NG1 5GL	0602 413313

WEST MIDLANDS REGION

Birmingham & Solihull	15th & 16th Floors Metropolitan House 1 Hagley Road Birmingham B16 8TG	021-456 1199
Coventry & Warwickshire	5th & 6th Floors Bankfield House 163 New Union Street Coventry CV1 2QQ	0203 631133
Dudley & Sandwell	6th Floor Falcon House The Minories Dudley DY2 8PG	0384 455391
Staffordshire	Moorlands House, Trinity Street Hanley Stoke on Trent ST1 5LN	0782 262131
The Marches Hereford/ Worcester	2nd Floor Hazledene House Central Square Telford TF3 4JJ	0952 291471
Wolverhampton & Walsall	2nd Floor 30 Market Street Wolverhampton WV1 3AF	0902 311111

NORTHERN REGION

Cleveland	Corporation House, 73 Albert Road Middlesbrough TS1 2RU	0642 231023
County Durham	Valley Street North, Darlington DL1 1TJ	0325 51166
Northumberland North Tyneside & Newcastle	1st Floor Broadacre House Market Street Newcastle upon Tyne NE1 6HH	091-232 6181
Sunderland South Tyneside & Gateshead	Derwent House Washington New Town NE38 7ST	091-416 6161

NORTH WEST REGION

Cheshire	1st Floor Spencer House Dewhurst Road Birchwood Centre Warrington WA3 7PP	0925 826515
Cumbria	1st & 2nd Floors Thirlmere Building 50 Lakes Road Derwent Howe Workington CA14 3YB	0900 66991
Lancashire	3rd Floor Duchy House 96 Lancaster Road Preston PR1 1HE	0772 59393
Central Manchester	4th & 5th Floors Boulton House 17-21 Chorlton Street Manchester M1 3HY	061-236 7222
Greater Manchester North	3rd Floor Provincial House Nelson Square Bolton BL1 1PN	0204 397350
Manchester East	1st Floor 1 St Peter's Square Stockport SK1 1NN	061-477 8830
Merseyside	4th Floor Sefton House Exchange Street East Liverpool L2 3XR	051-236 0026

SCOTLAND

Ayrshire, Dumfries & Galloway	25 Bank Street Kilmarnock KA1 1ER	0563 44044
Central & Fife	5 Kirk Loan Corstorphine Edinburgh EH12 7HD	031-334 9821
Glasgow City	4th Floor George House 36 North Hanover Street Glasgow G1 2AD	041-552 3411
Grampian & Tayside	4th & 5th Floors Argyll House Marketgait Dundee DD1 1UD	0382 29971

Highlands & Islands	3rd Floor Metropolitan House 31-33 High Street Inverness IV1 1TX	0463 220555
Lanarkshire	1st Floor Scomagg House Crosshill Street Motherwell ML1 1RU	0698 51411
Lothian & Borders	Orchard Brae House 30 Queensferry Road Edinburgh EH4 2HS	031-315 2888
Renfrewshire Dumbarton & Argyll	West Block 5 Elm Bank Gardens Charing Cross Glasgow G2 4PN	041-226 5544

SOUTH EAST REGION

Berkshire & Oxfordshire	5th Floor Kings Point 120 Kings Road Reading RG1 3BZ	0734 586262
Buckinghamshire & Hertfordshire	2nd Floor 31 Octagon Parade High Wycombe HP11 2LD	0494 33473
Essex	Globe House New Street Chelmsford CM1 1UG	0245 358548
Hampshire & Isle of Wight	25 Thackeray Mall Fareham Shopping Centre Fareham PO16 0PQ	0329 285924
Kent	5th Floor Mountbatten House 28 Military Road Chatham ME4 4JE	0634 44411
Surrey	Technology House 48-54 Goldsworth Road Woking GU21 1LE	0486 228190
Sussex	Gresham House 12-24 Station Road Crawley RH10 1HT	0293 562922

SOUTH WEST REGION

Avon	PO Box 164	0272 277116
	4th Floor	
	Minster House	
	27 Baldwin Street	
	Bristol BS99 7HR	
Devon &	6th Floor	0752 671671
Cornwall	Intercity House	
	Plymouth Station	
	Plymouth	
	PL4 6AA	
Dorset &	Crescent	0823 259121
Somerset	House	
	The Mount	
	Taunton	
	TA1 3TT	
Gloucestershire	Conway House	0452 24488
& Wiltshire	33-35 Worcester Street	
	Gloucester GL1 3AJ	

WALES

Dyfed & West	3rd Floor	0792 460355
Glamorgan	Orchard House	
	Orchard Street	
	Swansea SA1 5AP	
Gwent	Government	0633 56161
	Building	
	Cardiff Road	
	Newport	
	NP9 1YE	
Gwynedd, Clwyd	Wynnstay	0978 290333
& Powys	Block	
	Hightown Barracks	
	Kingsmill Road	
	Wrexham LL13 8BH	
Mid & South	5th Floor	0222 755744
Glamorgan	Phase One Building	
	Ty Glas Road	
	Llanishen	
	Cardiff CF4 5PJ	

YORKSHIRE & HUMBERSIDE REGION

Bradford	5th Floor	0274 723711
Calderdale &	Provincial House	
Kirklees	Tyrell Street	
	Bradford BD1 5NP	
Humberside	4th Floor	0482 226491
	Essex House	
	Manor Street	
	Hull HU1 1YA	
North Yorkshire	Fairfax House	0532 446181
& Leeds	Merrion Street	
	Leeds LS2 8JU	
Sheffield &	8th Floor	0742 701911
Rotherham	Sheaf House	
	The Pennine Centre	
	Hawley Street	
	Sheffield S1 3GA	
Wakefield	York House	0532 450502
Doncaster &	31-36 York Place	
Barnsley	Leeds LS1 2EB	

Fig. 5.2 DTI regional contacts

DTI North-East
Cleveland, Durham,
Northumberland, Tyne & Wear.
Consultancy Initiatives:
091-235 7292
Other Initiatives:
091-232 4722
Stanegate House
2 Groat Market
Newcastle upon Tyne NE1 1YN

DTI North-West (Manchester)
Cheshire (except Chester)
Cumbria, Lancashire, Greater
Manchester and the High Peak
District of Derbyshire.
All Initiatives:
061-838 5000
75 Mosley Street
Manchester M2 3HR

DTI North-West (Liverpool)
Liverpool, Widnes/Runcorn,
Wirral/Chester, and St. Helens/
Wigan.
All Initiatives:
051-224 6300
Graeme House
Derby Square
Liverpool L2 7UP

DTI Yorkshire and Humberside
North Yorkshire, South
Yorkshire, West Yorkshire and
Humberside.
Consultancy Initiatives:
0532 338300
Regional Enterprise Grants:
0532 338360
Other Initiatives:
0532 443171
Priestley House
3-5 Park Row
Leeds LS1 5LF

DTI East Midlands
Nottinghamshire, Derbyshire
(except the High Peak District),
Leicestershire, Lincolnshire and
Northamptonshire.
Consultancy Initiatives:
0602 596460
Regional Enterprise Grants:
0602 596475
Other Initiatives:
0602 506181
Severns House
20 Middle Pavement
Nottingham NG1 7DW

DTI West Midlands
The metropolitan districts of
Birmingham, Coventry, Dudley,
Sandwell, Solihull, Walsall and
Wolverhampton, and the
counties of Warwickshire,
Staffordshire, Shropshire, and
Hereford and Worcester.
All Initiatives:
021-631 6181
Ladywood House
Stephenson Street
Birmingham B2 4DT

DTI South-East (London)
Greater London.
Consultancy Initiatives:
01-627 7800
Export Initiative:
01-215 0574
*Research and Technology
Initiative:*
01-215 0557
*Enterprise and Education
Initiative:*
01-215 0564
Other Initiatives:
01-215 0572
Bridge Place
88/89 Eccleston Square
London SW1V 1PT

DTI South-East (Cambridge)
Bedfordshire, Cambridgeshire,
Essex, Hertfordshire, Norfolk, Suffolk.
All Initiatives:
Cambridge 0223 461939
The Westbrook Centre
Milton Road
Cambridge CB4 1YG

DTI South-East (Reading)
Berkshire, Buckinghamshire,
Hampshire, Oxfordshire and
Isle of Wight.
All Initiatives:
Reading 0734 395600
40 Caversham Road
Reading RG1 7EB

DTI South-East (Reigate)
Kent, Surrey, and Sussex.
All Initiatives:
0737 226900
Douglas House
40 London Road
Reigate RH2 9QP

DTI South-West
Avon, Cornwall (including
Scilly Isles), Devon, Dorset,
Gloucestershire, Somerset
and Wiltshire.
Consultancy Initiatives:
0272 308400
Regional Enterprise Grants:
0736 60440
Other Initiatives:
0272 272666
The Pithay
Bristol BS1 2PB

Scotland: Scottish Office
All Initiatives:
041-248 4774
Industry Department for
Scotland
Alhambra House
Waterloo Street
Glasgow G2 6AT

Wales
Consultancy Initiatives:
0443 841777 (24 hour
answering service)
Enterprise Initiative Section
Welsh Development Agency
Business Development Centre
Treforest Industrial Estate
nr Pontypridd
Mid Glamorgan CF37 5UT

Mid Wales
Dial 100 and ask for
Freefone New Wales
Business Advisory Service
Mid Wales Development
Ladywell House
Newtown
Mid Wales SY16 1JB
All other Initiatives:
0222 823185 (24 hour
answering service)
Welsh Office Industry
Department
New Crown Buildings
Cathays Park
Cardiff CF1 3NQ

Fig. 5.3 Advice from the Small Firms Service
Courtesy: *The Small Firms Service*

The Small Firms Service

With twelve main centres and over 80 additional offices around the country, the Small Firms Service is run by the Training Agency with the aim of providing advice to small businesses and people hoping to start a business. The service is extremely useful as a first stop for advice and is usually very good about knowing what's available in your local area. They can tell you of any managed workshop schemes in your locality, any training courses, any local authority help for small businesses, etc. They also offer a business development service for established small firms and a free information service. For more complex matters you can make an appointment for a counselling session. The first three days' consultancy are free, so it is well worth trying them out before you pay for professional advice.

If you want to get in touch with the Small Firms Service you should ring the operator and ask for *Freefone Enterprise*. You will be put through to your closest branch of the Small Firms Service and the call will cost you nothing.

The Small Firms Service covers the whole of England and different bodies exist to provide a similar service in other parts of the UK. To discover your closest office or to ask for details of the help available contact the appropriate head office:

Scotland
The Scottish Development Agency, Small Business Division, Rosebury House, Haymarket Terrace, Edinburgh EH12 5EZ. Tel: 031 337 9595.

Or:
The Highlands and Islands Development Board, Bridge House, 27 Bank St, Inverness IV1 1QR. Tel: 0463 234171.

Wales
The Welsh Development Agency, Small Business Unit, Treforest Industrial Estate, Pontypridd CF37 5UT. Tel: 0443 852666.

Northern Ireland
The Local Enterprise Development Unit (LEDU), Lamont House, Purdy's Lane, Newtownbreda, Belfast BT8 4TB. Tel: 0232 691031.

The Rural Development Commission

The Rural Development Commission (formerly CoSIRA) was set up to provide help to manufacturing and service industries (but not agriculture) in the countryside and in small towns with less than 10 000 inhabitants. The RDC offers some valuable assistance including:

a local advice
b help with premises
c professional consultancy
d technical help
e loans

If your planned location is in a rural area or a small town the RDC could turn out to be your most useful source of assistance. Look in the telephone directory under Rural Development Commission to see if there is a branch near you. If you can't find one you could contact the head office:

Rural Development Commission, 141 Castle St, Salisbury SP1 3PT. Tel: 0722 336255.

Local Enterprise Agencies

Local Enterprise Agencies are often funded by large companies and staffed by people seconded from those companies. Some are supported by local authorities. Their aim is to provide help and advice to local small businesses. Services may vary from one agency to another but in general they offer:

a training courses in business management
b help with finding suitable premises
c assistance with raising finance

There are now around 300 Local Enterprise Agencies spread all over the country. You can find out which is closest to you by contacting:

Business in the Community, 227A City Rd, London EC1V 1JU. Tel: 01 253 3716.

Small Business Clubs

A Small Business Club is not a source of assistance in the formal sense of the term, but joining one could certainly be very useful to anyone starting a business. A Small Business Club will usually have monthly meetings which are addressed by a speaker on a specialist business topic, followed by a general social get together. Meeting people who already have their own small business is both interesting and useful. You can ask members for the name of a good accountant, discuss problems, find out where to obtain supplies, hear about premises which could be coming onto the market and maybe meet some potential customers. There will probably be a Small Business Club somewhere near to you. You can find out by contacting your local Small Firms Service office.

The Small Firms Loan Guarantee Scheme

This scheme is designed to help small firms with a good idea but no track record or security to offer, to raise finance. A new business which is not able to borrow money by conventional means from the bank may be able to borrow the money under the government-backed Loan Guarantee Scheme. This source of help is covered in more detail in Chapter 12.

Help from British Steel

BSC (Industry) Ltd is a separate company formed by the British Steel Corporation with the aim of helping the growth of new businesses to replace some of the jobs which have been lost in steel closure areas. Help is available to anyone, not just British Steel employees, and includes:

a unsecured loans at attractive rates of interest
b help with employing staff
c help with training staff
d premises

It is a very attractive package but it is available only to businesses located in steel closure areas. Further details can be obtained from:

BSC (Industry) Ltd, NLA Tower, 12 Addiscombe Rd, Croydon CR9 3JH. Tel: 01 686 0366.

Enterprise Zones

Enterprise Zones have been created by the government with the aim of stimulating business development in areas of high unemployment. They hope to achieve this by removing some of the costs and red tape which have maybe deterred people from starting or expanding businesses in the past. There are only two real benefits for the new small business: exemption from rates on business premises for ten years from the date of the creation of the Enterprise Zone; and relaxation and simplification of planning regulations, which could be helpful if you needed 'change of use' planning permission for your premises (see Chapter 6).

However, most Enterprise Zone benefits are of use mainly to large companies or to property developers because they take the form of significant incentives for the building of new industrial premises. Unfortunately, practice seems to show that few, if any, of these financial benefits are then passed on to the man who rents the premises. In general, Enterprise Zones benefit the business which starts with high capital investment.

Further information on Enterprise Zones can be obtained from the Small Firms Service or:

The Department of the Environment, 2 Marsham St, London SW1P 3EB. Tel: 01 212 7158.

Regional aid

Help is also available in certain areas of the country under the government's regional aid programme. Grants are no longer automatic, but may include:

a long rent free periods (up to two years in some cases)
b grants for industrial property building or alterations
c grants for the purchase of new machinery
d help with training staff
e selective financial assistance for new projects

It is fair to say that once again the real value of the packages on offer in assisted areas may well prove disappointing to very small new businesses. Generally speaking, the larger the company and the more people it can employ, the greater its chance of receiving regional aid.

However, if you want more detailed information about the availability of regional aid in your area contact the Small Firms Service or:

The Department of Trade and Industry, 66-74 Victoria St, London SW1E 6SJ. Tel: 01 212 3466.

Inner urban areas

The Inner Urban Areas Act of 1978 gave some local authorities the power to assist new businesses in a number of ways:

a loans or grants for property improvements

b loans or grants towards the setting up of workers' cooperatives

In 'special inner urban areas' there may also be additional assistance such as:

a help with rent

b help with installing services, such as electricity, in your premises

Help available under the Inner Urban Aid programme is often genuinely useful to the typical small business. You may find managed workshop schemes funded under this programme and if you are thinking of starting a workers' cooperative the help could be particularly useful. If you would like further details of the potential assistance available under the Inner Urban Aid programme you should contact the Small Firms Service or:

The Department of the Environment, Inner Urban Aid Programme, 2 Marsham St, London SW1P 3EB. Tel: 01 212 7158.

New towns

New Town Development Corporations can offer selective assistance to new businesses over and above any other regional aid that may be available. There should be a good range of new factory units available but the size of premises and the package of incentives on offer will often favour the larger than average new business because it will employ quite a few staff from the outset. However, if a 'new town' is conveniently located for your purposes it would be foolish not to find out what is on offer. Check with your local Small Firms Service or with:

The New Towns Association, Metro House, 58 St. James St, London SW1Y 5BL. Tel: 01 930 2631.

Help for new technology

There is considerable government interest at the moment in encouraging manufacturing industry to invest in new technology. A whole range of incentives are available for companies who are prepared to do this. You will probably find that most of these schemes are beyond the limited means of the average new business but if you are starting a manufacturing business with a fairly high capital input and you have plant and equipment to buy, you may find some valuable financial support is available to you. For further details contact:

The Department of Trade and Industry, Ashdown House, 123 Victoria St, London SW1E 6RB. Tel: 01 212 7676.

Help in London

If you will be starting your business in London there are some additional and especially useful sources of help available to you.

The London Enterprise Agency (LENTA)

Founded in 1979 by a group of large companies, the aim of LENTA is to help the creation of new small businesses in London. Assistance includes:

a advice
b training
c help with raising finance

LENTA has been widely acknowledged as a most valuable source of help for new business in London and would be well worth approaching. The address is:

The London Enterprise Agency, 69 Cannon St, London EC4N 5AB. Tel: 01 248 4444.

The London Docklands Development Corporation

This body is redeveloping the old docklands area at a very quick rate and has become a major provider of premises for small businesses in London. Assistance with rent and other premises costs should be available. For details contact:

The London Docklands Development Corporation, West India House, Millwall Dock, London E14 9TJ. Tel: 01 515 3000.

Summary

1 The Enterprise Allowance Scheme is a very useful source of financial help for many new business people.

2 Those people receiving benefit may be able to take some steps towards starting their new business without losing their benefit rights.

3 Valuable training and consultancy assistance is available through the Training Agency and DTI.

4 The Small Firms Service will be the most useful source of advice for most new businesses but the RDC, Local Enterprise Agencies and Small Business Clubs should all be investigated as potentially helpful organizations.

5 Certain areas offer additional forms of assistance to businesses. Although some are disappointing in practice to small businesses it is well worth checking exactly what is available in your planned area of location.

6 Additional financial help may be available to manufacturing businesses, particularly those dealing in new technology.

7 Special help is available to new businesses in the London area.

6 Location and premises

Aims of this chapter

This chapter will examine four areas that may play a critical role in the success of your business over the years ahead:

- Choosing the right location to best serve the needs of your customers
- Determining the type of premises that would be most appropriate for your kind of business
- Avoiding potential problems in acquiring business premises
- The possible option of working from home

Choosing the right location

'Location, location, location.'

According to Conrad Hilton, the world famous hotelier, these are the three main factors that determine the success of a business! However, many people starting a new business ignore the question of location completely. Large companies do not make that mistake. They devote a considerable proportion of their planning time to planning their location because they know that unless their business is situated in the location that enables it to provide the best possible service to its customers, they will lose out to those competitors who are better located. The factors involved in choosing the best possible location for a new small business are:

1 Convenience for you. If you're going to run a successful business you will soon have to get used to the idea that convenience for your customers is much more important that convenience for yourself. However, you have to be practical about this and must also take account of the genuine constraints which may restrict your choice of location. It's no use doing all your research and homework only to discover that the ideal location for your business is the south coast of Cornwall when family considerations would prevent you from moving more than twenty miles from Sheffield! Your first job is to decide what your personal and family constraints are.

2 Convenience for your customers. This is of paramount importance if you are planning to open a wine bar, an off licence, a hairdressing salon, a car repair workshop or a retail shop. If you will be dependent on customers coming to you, it is vital that your business is located in the kind of place that your customers already frequent.

So your first step is to decide **who** your customers are, **where** they are, and **which locations** would therefore be most convenient and/or most attractive to them. If you are selling basic goods or services the emphasis will be on convenience. If you are selling leisure goods, or more expensive, less frequently purchased items, you can afford to consider locations which would prove attractive to your kind of customers. People would not drive 25 miles to buy a bag of chips, but they would for an expensive meal in a rural, country house setting. Thus although you may not need an expensive prime site on the high street, you should be very careful about saving money on premises if it means opting for a location which your customers might find inconvenient.

3 Closeness to your market. Even if your customers will not normally visit your premises you will probably still need to be close to them. Your customers will value prompt deliveries, maybe at short notice. They may want you to visit them to answer technical queries or to provide after sales service. Your ability to cater for your customers' needs in this way may give you a competitive edge over your rivals in the market. If transport costs are significant you may make large savings from being close to your customers.

4 Availability of suitable labour. If the success of your business is dependent on the employment of suitable staff, then the availability of people with suitable skills should be a significant factor in your location decision. Even if you are not going to employ many people initially but expect to do so within two or three years if all goes well, you should investigate the availability of suitable labour now, at the planning stage.

The best source of information on the availability of labour in specific areas of skill would be the Training Agency area office. You could also try talking to the local Jobcentre or the local chamber of commerce.

Even if you will only be employing unskilled staff, location could be important. If you were to locate your business too far out in the wilds, somewhere accessible only by car, you might be severely restricting your ability to recruit staff, especially part-time staff.

5 Closeness to suppliers. You need to ensure that your business is located in an area where you can rely on regular deliveries of important supplies, and where the terms of delivery will be the same as they are for your competitors in other areas. You don't want to put yourself at a price disadvantage relative to your competitors. If you will be manufacturing you will find that the regular delivery of supplies and the ability to get supplies at short notice (even if you have to go and collect them yourself) will be absolutely essential to the smooth and profitable running of your business.

6 Regional inducements. If you can satisfy all the other location criteria and still take advantage of the short-term financial incentives offered in one of the assisted areas, you can regard it as a bonus. However, it would be very short-sighted to place regional inducements above the other criteria in importance. They might be of great help initially if you are short of starting up capital, but if locating in an assisted area might put your business at a competitive disadvantage in the long run you would effectively be committing suicide on behalf of your business if you located there.

Once you have drawn up your location priorities you can start to hunt for premises in areas which fit in with your guidelines.

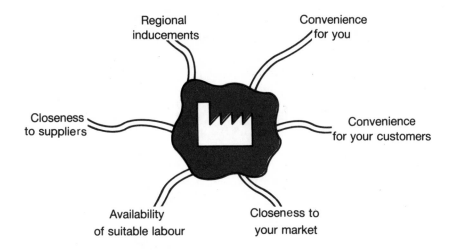

Fig. 6.1 Factors influencing the location of your small business

Decisions about premises

There are a lot of difficult decisions to get right about premises and a lot of dangerous traps that the inexperienced can very easily fall into. The aim of this section will be to go through the process of looking for, evaluating, and occupying business premises, highlighting the potential dangers and offering some practical advice.

Finding business premises

Since your premises will have such an enormous impact on the efficiency of the business, will form such a large part of your costs, and may have a great effect on the image of the business and its ability to attract customers, you must be prepared to devote a lot of time, effort and a certain amount of money to making sure that you acquire information about all the opportunities for business premises in your area. There are a number of ways of gaining this information:

1 **Estate agents.** The obvious answer, but not necessarily a very useful source of information. Many estate agents will have few, if any, commercial or industrial premises on their books. They are more likely to have retail properties. However, you must visit all the local estate agents just in case they do have something of interest and ask to be put on their mailing list. In larger towns you will find agents who specialize in commercial property, and they should prove more useful.

2 **Commercial publications.** In some parts of the country you may find the commercial and industrial property pages of publications like *Dalton's Weekly* or *Estates Gazette* quite useful.

3 **Local newspapers.** Virtually all local newspapers carry a certain amount of property advertising. Many small offices, shops or workshops available for rental will be advertised privately by the owner in the local newspaper rather than involving an estate agent. Many will just be small ads, so it is essential to wade through them all every week.

4 **Advisory bodies.** If there are any small business advisory organizations in your area such as an Enterprise Agency, a business venture, RDC, etc, they could prove to be a useful source of information about premises available in the locality. Your local council may have an industrial development or economic development department which could also provide you with information.

5 **Walking the streets.** Why not have a look around yourself? If your location studies have led you to the conclusion that a particular small area is your best or only possible location, it would probably be worthwhile having a look around the area to see if there are any empty premises which look suitable for your purposes. Find out who owns them and make an approach. You may be lucky enough to find someone who has more space than he needs who is very pleased with the idea of earning some money by renting out his surplus.

Is it better to rent or buy?

It is often taken for granted that buying premises is better than renting them. Although it is unlikely that owning your business premises would be a bad investment, using your capital in other ways may be a much better investment. If you are in business to make as much profit as possible you should buy rather than rent property only if it will increase your profits. Tax considerations could also be important if you are contemplating buying property, so your accountant should definitely be consulted.

The advantages of *owning* premises are:

1 Control. A freehold property is yours to extend, alter, paint, decorate and generally improve when it suits you and the needs of your business. You would not be dependent on the agreement of the landlord, and of course any increase in the value of the property as a result of the improvements would be for your benefit.

2 Financial planning. If you own property, your mortgage repayments will tend to decrease in real terms as the years go by. Rented property will no doubt be subject to regular rent increases. Buying may therefore be cheaper in the long run. However you should be aware that interest rates may fluctuate, and thus your repayments could increase in the short term.

3 Building up capital. The capital which accumulates in property can be particularly useful for a small business owner when he comes to retirement.

4 Security. A major advantage is the ability to use the business property as security for a loan which could be far preferable to pledging personal assets, provided, of course, you do have some personal equity in the property.

The advantages of *renting* premises are:

1 Liquidity. As you are almost certain to have to pay at least a ten per cent deposit buying property takes up a lot of capital which could otherwise be available for other start-up requirements of your business.

2 Borrowing money. Until you have paid some money off your property loan the net value of the property will probably be insufficient to offer as security for a bank loan. Also, if you use up a lot of your borrowing power for buying property you may not have the ability to raise finance for other business requirements.

3 Depreciation. It is possible for property to depreciate as well as appreciate in value due to environmental or economic factors beyond your control. If an area becomes run down or if the demand for industrial property falls you could find yourself stuck with a depreciating asset which would be very difficult to sell. This is not a major risk, but it is a greater danger with business property than it is with domestic property.

4 Legal costs. Buying property is bound to involve higher legal costs than renting premises, which would put a further strain on your start-up capital.

5 Expansion. If your business expands rapidly at first you could soon outgrow your first premises. If this is a possibility you would be wise to rent premises at first.

Evaluating business premises

Nobody would buy their raw materials for manufacture or their stock for retailing from a supplier who charged 15 per cent over the odds. So why should it be any different spending more on your premises than you need to? A lot of people starting their first business leave the search for premises much too late. As a result they rush into the first empty premises they find which may be unsuitable and expensive. Therefore you must spend the time now, at the planning stage, researching premises so that you will be able to make a good decision when you do eventually commit yourself.

During your early investigations into premises you should concentrate on two issues: do the premises meet the needs of the business; and do they represent good value for money?

1 Do the premises meet the needs of the business? There follow some ideas for the kind of points that you might want to bear in mind when looking at premises:

a Size. Machinery, equipment, storage space all have a habit of taking up more room than you expect. It would be a good idea to draw a plan on graph paper, to scale, showing premises of a certain size, and draw in all your business equipment. The size of premises you require might turn out to be larger than you think.

b Height. Some businesses need height to work in. For others it would be a disadvantage to have a high ceiling because the premises might be too difficult to heat.

c Floor. Is the floor strong enough to take any of your heavy machinery?

d Security. If there will be a lot of valuable stock or equipment inside the building, security could be a very important point.

e Parking. For yourself, your employees, your customers.

f Access. Deliveries of supplies could be made by very large lorries, so the access for them will need to be adequate.

g Heating and lighting. Are they adequate for your purposes?

h Services. Are all the services that you need available, including three phase electricity if you will have machinery, and gas, water, sewerage, telephone, rubbish removal, toilets and hand washing facilities?

i Office space. You may just want a workshop, but even a very small separate office will be very useful in the long run. If you try to do your administration in the workshop it will end up being very inefficient; it would be even worse to have all your paperwork at home some miles away. You also need somewhere quiet to use the telephone, otherwise it can create a very bad impression with customers.

2 Are the premises good value for money? Before you can decide whether or not the premises represent good value for money you have to work out exactly how much they cost. This involves a lot more than simply the rent. Some people occupy business premises and are surprised by extra costs that they didn't know anything about six or even twelve months later. Costs may include:

a Rent. As well as the annual rent you ought to know how much rent you are paying per square foot. This is very useful when you are trying to compare premises of differing sizes. If the building is 32 feet long by 26 feet wide (832 sq. ft.) and the rent is £1872 per annum it means that the rent is £2.25 per square foot. As a further guide you can probably find out what the going rate is in the area for other workshops, offices, shops, etc, and make a comparison.

b Buildings insurance. The landlord normally insures the buildings. This may be part of the rent or it may be extra. If it is extra, it is essential, before signing a lease, to get a written quotation from the landlord for the annual cost of the building's insurance. It could be a lot more than you expect!

c Maintenance. You need to have it clearly explained to you exactly how much of the maintenance of the property will be your responsibility and how much will be the responsibility of the landlord. Normally the tenant would be responsible for the internal decoration and equipment (toilets, for example), and the landlord would be responsible for external maintenance and the fabric of the building. If you have any responsibility for external maintenance it could prove to be very expensive, so it is wise to have the property checked by a qualified surveyor before signing the lease.

d Communal estate charges. These are very popular little extras with the owners of industrial estates and may cover anything from sewers to landscaping. You must obtain a written quotation of the cost of these services.

If you quantify all the costs that have been mentioned so far, that total could be said to represent the real rent for the premises. You would get a more valid comparison figure by working out the **real rent per square foot** for different premises.

Charges may also be payable to other organizations:

a Rates. If the premises are not new it should be possible to find out the rates from the previous tenant, otherwise you would have to contact the District Council.

b Water rates. Water rates are separate from and additional to general rates.

c Contents insurance. The premium you have to pay to insure your contents could vary considerably between one property and another. To have a true comparison of the cost of occupying different properties, you need to get a quote for contents insurance from an insurance broker. (For more details of insurance see Chapter 7).

Item	Premises		
	A	B	C
Rent			
Buildings insurance			
Maintenance costs			
Communal charges			
Rates			
Water rates			
Contents insurance			
Heating			
Total annual cost £			
Cost per sq. ft. £			

Fig. 6.2 Premises – annual running costs

d Heating and ventilation. The cost of heating a building can vary enormously from one property to another. If your business will necessitate a certain minimum temperature because of the process or materials you will be using, your heating bills could be considerable in the winter. You will therefore have to estimate the costs of heating different premises. The ideal thing would be to obtain accurate information from the previous occupant. Failing that you could maybe ask the occupant of similar neighbouring premises. If necessary you will just have to make an estimation, remembering that old buildings tend to be colder and tall buildings will obviously cost more to heat. Some managed workshop schemes (p. 105) may even include the cost of heating and lighting within the rent. This could save you a lot of money on your running costs.

You could draw up a chart similar to the one opposite (fig. 6.2) to compare the annual cost of occupying different premises.

However, your property costs do not end here. There is also a considerable one-off cost when you occupy premises initially. These include:

a Lease premium. Sometimes, even when you are only renting rather than buying property, you have to make an initial lump sum payment for the lease. This is more common for shops than it is for industrial premises. It is well worth shopping around to find premises which do not involve an initial lump sum to buy the lease.

b Your own legal costs.

c The landlord's legal costs. It is not uncommon for the terms of the agreement to make the tenant responsible for the landlord's legal fees. If you have asked the landlord to put in writing to you any charges that you will be liable for in addition to the rent, then you will know if you are responsible for his legal fees.

d The landlord's estate agent's fees.

e Telephone installation. If there's no telephone you would have to check with British Telecom how much it would cost to have a business line installed. There may be a disconnected line in which case you would have to pay a reconnection charge.

f Power supply. New premises, particularly new industrial units, may not have had the power supply connected by the electricity board. This could be your responsibility and it could be another three figure bill.

g Internal electricity and lighting. Some industrial units may have a power supply, but that's all. They may have no lighting or electrical wiring whatsoever. To introduce electrical wiring, sockets and lighting installed by an electrician will not be cheap, so you would have to obtain some quotations.

h Decorating costs. If you are moving into retail or commercial premises you may need to decorate and generally spruce the place up in order to present the right impression to your customers.

i Conversion costs. Some businesses will need to modify premises to make them suitable. More extensive conversion work will probably require an estimate from a builder or other tradesmen.

Fig. 6.3 lays out another table of costs which will enable you to see just how much different premises would eat into your start-up capital. Sometimes the best premises for running costs turn out to be the worst for start-up costs. At least if you find out all the information to fill in both tables you will know exactly how much your premises would cost you. You must be realistic about the amount of your own time which might be absorbed by decorating or conversion. You should ask yourself whether that time would be better spent on activities more central to your business.

Item	Premises		
	A	B	C
Premium for lease			
Your own legal costs			
The landlord's legal and/or estate agent costs			
Telephone installation			
Power supply			
Internal electrics and lighting			
Decorating costs			
Conversion costs			
Total starting up cost £			
Cost per sq. ft. £			

Fig. 6.3 Premises – initial starting up costs

Regulations concerning business premises

Having identified your ideal premises it is essential to check that it will conform to certain rules and regulations.

1 Planning permission. Any building which is used for industrial or commercial purposes has to have planning permission. You may be tempted to assume that because a manufacturing company was the previous occupant of the premises and because you will be starting a manufacturing business, the premises must be approved. Not necessarily! There are two potential pitfalls. Firstly, for all you know the premises may never have had planning permission, and secondly, even if they have, it may not be planning permission which covers the particular activity which your business will be engaged in. Planning permission is very specific, so it is more than likely that you will have to apply at least for 'change of use' permission. So the first step is to approach the planning department of your District Council and find out if you need to apply for planning permission. If there is no problem you must get this confirmed in writing by the planning department. In some cases, an industrial estate, for example, it will be a mere formality quickly dispensed with, but in a mixed residential/industrial area it could be more of a problem and in a solely residential area you could have a really difficult job on your hands.

The first step is to invite the planning officer along to your proposed premises and explain your plans thoroughly to him. He will be able to give you his opinion of your chances of gaining planning permission, and should give you some advice about filling in the planning application. He will know the best way to present a case to the planning committee.

a Making the planning application. You need to get the correct application forms from the planning department of the District Council, fill them in, preferably with the help of the planning officer, attach any relevant drawings or plans, and include a cheque for the fee, which is currently about £70. It will probably be about six weeks before you get the result.

There are a number of additional measures you could take to support your case. It would be a very good idea to write to your local councillor explaining your plans to start a business, telling him about your planning application and inviting him to view the premises with you. If you can get him on your side he could be a useful ally. If you have any reason to believe that the application will be controversial, for instance, if the premises are in a largely residential area, you would be well advised to take additional measures to support your application. Quite how far you go will depends on how important it is for you to get these particular premises. If you have a good second choice of premises available you may not even think its worth paying £70 to secure the change of use (see if the landlord will pay it). On the other hand, if you consider particular premises to be vital to the success of your business it will be worth making a considerable effort to try to ensure the success of your planning application.

One of the most useful things you can do is to drum up popular support for your plans. Your objective would be to get as many people as possible to voice their support of your application with the planning committee. Get everybody you can think of to write on your behalf, including pressure groups such as the chamber of commerce, other local businesses and individuals, especially anybody who lives in the vicinity of your proposed premises. If you will be employing staff, you should tell your supporters to stress your business's potential role in reducing unemployment in the area. Conversely, if you know of any specific individuals who oppose your proposals it is essential to go and speak to them in person. If they have any misconceptions you should be able to put them right.

b Planning appeals. If your planning application is rejected you can appeal. The first step is to make a second application with a few modifications. Contact the planning officer and find out exactly why the application was unsuccessful. He may be on your side and may suggest a form of rewording that would help your case, or you may have to alter your plans slightly. You should then resubmit the application with a letter explaining the changes you have made.

If this still fails you can appeal to the Department of the Environment in London. The premises will have to be very important to your plans to justify all this commitment of time and money – such an appeal could easily cost £500 to £1000. At this stage you really do need a good expert adviser such as a solicitor who specializes in this field.

c Types of planning consent. There are three different categories of planning consent. The first, **full planning consent,** means that the premises can be used indefinitely for the use specified. If the premises change hands the planning consent is unaffected. The second, **temporary planning consent,** will have a time limit, which is usually between one and five years. If it is a short time limit it will affect your commitment to the premises in terms of the amount of money you want to spend on modifications. The third, **personal planning consent,** restricts the use of the premises to you personally. Any subsequent occupiers of the premises would have to reapply. This is fine in itself as far as you are concerned, but it will often be granted in conjunction with temporary planning consent.

2 Health and safety. All business premises are covered by the Health and Safety at Work Act of 1974, the Factories Act of 1961 or by the Offices, Shops and Railway Premises Act of 1963. Most of these regulations will be concerned with the way you run your business once it is started, but it may be that certain alterations would need to be made to your premises in order to make them safe in the eyes of the Inspectorate. This could be very costly so it makes sense to ask the opinion of the Health and Safety Inspector before you commit yourself to the premises. You should contact the local branch of the Health and Safety Executive and arrange for one of their Inspectors to meet you at the premises. They will be only too pleased to do this. If you don't know where your local office is you could find out from:

The Health and Safety Executive, 25 Chapel St, London NW1 5DT. Tel: 01 262 3277.

The Health and Safety Executive deals mainly with factories. Offices and shops tend to be covered by the Environmental Health Department of the District Council. When you start your business you will have to notify them and fill in a form OSR1 (unless you are self-employed and don't employ any staff). It is wise for anybody planning to occupy office or shop accommodation to contact the Environmental Health Department first, because if the premises should require expensive alterations you need to know this now. If your business is concerned with the preparation of food it is particularly important to do this.

3 **Fire prevention.** Do the premises have a fire prevention certificate? If not, or if you would be changing the use of the building, you should contact the local Fire Prevention Officer and ask him to visit the premises. If you break the fire regulations he could close your business down without notice.

4 **Security.** It is also worth evaluating the security of the premises. Does it have a burglar alarm? Do the windows and doors have appropriate protection? The insurance premium will be related to security so you could find yourself having to pay higher premiums for some premises.

Signing the lease

If the premises have passed all the tests that have been covered so far you will be ready to sign the lease. On the whole you would be well advised to use a solicitor to handle this for you, although there are some premises, usually managed workshops schemes (see page 105) which have very simple agreements which you could safely sign without the cost of using a solicitor. If you are unsure, consult one of the local sources of free advice first (the Small Firms Service, for example). However complex or simple the lease there are some important issues that you should want to clarify.

a The term of the lease. How long does it last? The longer it lasts the longer you are responsible for paying the rent. It is true that a long lease gives you more security in that the landlord can't remove you as long as you conform to the terms of the lease, but for some new businesses even two years is a long time to look ahead. A short lease may therefore be more appropriate for many new businesses just starting out.

b Personal guarantees. If you have formed a company for the protection of limited liability you should try to avoid any lease which makes you personally responsible for anything. The lease should be in the name of the company.

c Rent increases. If the lease makes provision for rent increases you should make sure that these increases are controlled in a way that you find acceptable. A clause which simply enables the landlord to increase the rent at certain intervals should not be accepted. It is much better if future rent increases are based on a pre-determined yardstick, such as the rate of inflation.

d Deposits. You should fight very hard against paying a deposit. When you leave it could be very hard to get it back. If the lease has a clause which binds you to leave the premises in a decent state of repair and decoration you should argue that there is no need for you to pay a deposit as well.

e Rent-free period. It is very common now for a rent-free period to be granted to new tenants of industrial and commercial property. You may get as much as three months rent free if you are very lucky, but you should certainly hold out for at least one month rent free on the grounds that it will take you that long to move in and get everything set up before you can start trading.

f Payment intervals. It is easiest on the cash flow of a new business to have your payment intervals as short as possible. Some landlords like the rent to be paid quarterly in advance, which can mean that you have a very big cheque to write out once every three months. Monthly payments are much more reasonable for a new business.

g Repairs and maintenance. It is normal and reasonable for the tenant to be responsible for the internal condition of the property and maybe regular external maintenance such as painting the woodwork. The fabric and structure of the building should be the landlord's responsibility.

Working from home

Plenty of people want to try out their business idea in a very low-risk way so that if they find they don't like running a business, or that customers don't like their product or services, they can cease trading with little harm done. Starting a business in a very small way from home, on a part-time basis, with very low start-up costs, and gradually expanding until it is running full-time before looking for new business premises may be a very sensible approach for many people to adopt.

The advantages of working from home are:

1 **Lower start-up costs.** Moving into business premises will always cost a fair amount of money so 'making do' at home with a bedroom and the garage would greatly reduce start-up costs.

2 **Lower risk.** If you work from home you will minimize your commitments and make it easier to cease trading if you decide that running a business is not for you.

3 **Saving time.** If you are starting your business on a part-time basis, working at home will help you to make more efficient use of your time.

4 **Overheads.** If you are starting your business in a small way at first, your turnover would probably be too small to support the additional overheads of separate business premises. If you use your home you would have no additional rent, rates, and telephone installation costs, and you would be able to offset a proportion of your household bills (excluding mortgage) against tax, but do consult an accountant on such matters.

5 **Office accommodation.** You may be starting a business which could operate in a perfectly satisfactory way from home for a long time, perhaps for ever. This would apply to many self-employed people such as plumbers, electricians, travelling hairdressers or anybody providing a service who visits their customers in their home or at their premises. In all these cases you would just be using your home as a base and a place to do paperwork. Unless you are going to employ staff and plan to expand the business you will probably find your home fulfils your business premises requirements quite acceptably.

The disadvantages of working from home are:

1 **Planning permission.** Strictly speaking you are acting against the law by using your home as business premises. Your home probably only has planning permission to be used as domestic premises and therefore you are supposed to apply for 'change of use' planning permission (as described in the previous section). However, most local authorities will turn a blind eye to businesses being run from people's homes provided the rules are not broken

in too blatant a manner. The crux of the matter is the fact that your neighbours in a residential area do not want the place turned into an industrial estate. Therefore if you do run your business from home:

a keep things as quiet as possible
b store any materials or equipment out of sight
c collect materials rather than have them delivered by big lorries
d discourage business callers at your home as far as possible
e don't burn smelly rubbish in the back garden!

All these things are common sense, but it doesn't stop some people from doing them and being genuinely surprised and upset when a neighbour complains! The chief disadvantage of working from home is that however careful you are you can never rule out the possibility of complaints, which would leave the council with no option but to order you to find alternative premises. It is therefore not a good idea to spend much money at all on making your home suitable for business use unless you have planning permission.

2 **Insurance.** Running your business from home could be risky as far as insurance is concerned. Storing flammable materials in your garage for example, as well as being a health and safety hazard, could invalidate your insurance. Even less obviously risky operations, such as carrying out dirty or dusty work, could be said to increase the risk of fire.

3 **Efficiency.** In the long run it may prove to be very inefficient working from home full-time if you have to spend a lot of time there, because there are always lots of distractions. A small workshop or office where you 'go to work' will probably be much more efficient.

4 **Image.** Although working from home is ideal for some businesses, such as service businesses, e.g. electricians, writers, designers, computer programmers, you should be alive to the possibility that if you run your business from home some customers might see you as a 'tin pot little outfit' unlikely to be professional enough to provide the service, quality or delivery they require.

In conclusion using your home is feasible as a short-term experiment for most new businesses, although if its going to be too offensive to neighbours or if there's any danger of burning the house down, it's not really a good idea! In the long run your home can only really be suitable for a very small part-time business or for the plumber or electrician type of business where your home would be used only as an address, a telephone point and a place to do your paperwork.

Managed workshops

It has always been difficult for new small businesses to find suitable premises to rent. The main problems are usually encountered by people who want very small premises for their new businesses and do not want to sign a long lease until they have tried things out and are certain that they are going along the right lines. However, there are now a growing number of premises, which will be referred to as 'managed workshops', which fulfil exactly this need.

What usually happens is that the local authority or a private organization takes over a large building, such as an old factory which has closed down, and converts it into lots of small starter units for new businesses. These units can range in size from 100 square feet to 2000 square feet. Although often called 'managed workshops' there is no standard name for such premises and you may see many different names used to describe them. Some of these names are: Enterprise Centre, New Enterprise Workshops, Innovation Centre, Industrial Centre, Business Centre, Managed Workshops, Managed Workspace, and Shared Workspace.

Some advantages of the managed workshops package are:

1 **Small units.** It can be extremely difficult to find premises that are small enough for your needs and budget. The availability of very small units in a managed workshop scheme is therefore a tremendous advantage.

2 **Little risk.** Units are usually available on terms which require only one month's notice for termination of the agreement.

3 **Communal office services.** Many managed workshop schemes have a large office with one or more secretaries who are available to do office work for the small businesses who have their premises within the scheme. Office services are usually available on a 'pay as you use' basis. It might cost you 50 pence to have a letter typed, for example. Each tenant business has its charges totted up and settles the bill at the end of the month. The kind of office services that might be available on a communal basis are:

  a typing services
  b photocopying
  c telephone answering
  d book-keeping
  e telex
  f letter franking
  g computing services
  h fax services

These services are extremely valuable for a new business which doesn't have much money. It saves you a lot on your start-up costs because you don't have to buy items like a typewriter or an answering machine. You don't need to worry about employing a secretary or spend a lot of time doing such work yourself. Above all it enables your business to prevent a very professional image right from the start, and that is something that you might find very difficult with just your own resources.

4 Advisory services. Some managed workshop schemes have 'in-house' advisory services of some kind. Very often this will be provided by the manager of the centre who may have been specially chosen for his wide business experience and his ability to advise new businesses. Having someone like this to turn to when problems arise is extremely valuable to any new business.

5 Training courses. Training courses in management skills may be provided on the premises either by the permanent staff or by outside organizations. Most new business owners need training, but many don't get round to doing anything about it. Having courses available on the spot makes it much easier for you to improve your business knowledge and skills.

6 Communal machine shop. If you were very lucky there might even be a communal machine shop, containing a selection of the commonly used engineering machines such as lathes, milling machines, grinders, etc, and available on a pay as you use basis to tenants. This can save you a vast amount of money on your start-up costs and, just as important, it could enable you to try things out which would have been impossible with just your own resources.

7 Few legal formalities. Units are usually available on monthly licenses which are very simple agreements and should not involve you in legal fees.

8 Relations with other businesses. There might be 50 to 100 small businesses in the same property. This means that you get to know a lot of other people in the same position as yourself. This is good for morale and good for business as tenants often trade with each other.

9 Growing room. Although the availability of very small premises is a real bonus when you first start, you may be starting to outgrow your 300 square feet within a few months if all goes well. In a managed workshop scheme there is usually a very good chance of finding slightly larger premises to move into, or additional units to take on as you grow.

10 Conference facilities. Some schemes have a communal room which tenants can hire for entertaining important customers, or putting on a small exhibition.

11 Refreshments. Some large schemes have a cafe where you can get meals and snacks throughout the working day. Even the small ones will have a communal hot drinks machine, and probably someone who comes round selling sandwiches at lunch time – his own small business!

12 Light and heat. Some schemes even have communal lighting and heating provided which you pay for as part of the rent. This probably doesn't save anything on running costs but might save you a lot on your start-up costs, since some new industrial units require you to install your own heating and lighting.

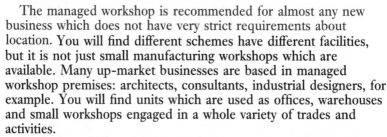 The managed workshop is recommended for almost any new business which does not have very strict requirements about location. You will find different schemes have different facilities, but it is not just small manufacturing workshops which are available. Many up-market businesses are based in managed workshop premises: architects, consultants, industrial designers, for example. You will find units which are used as offices, warehouses and small workshops engaged in a whole variety of trades and activities.

To find out if there are any such schemes in a convenient location for your business you could make enquiries through your local branch of the Small Firms Service or RDC, or contact your local council.

Summary

1 For some businesses a critical success factor will be the right choice of location. The more direct contact you will need with your customers, especially if they have to come to your premises, the more crucial the location decision.

2 A good location is one that is convenient for your customers rather than one which is convenient for yourself.

3 Suitable premises can be difficult to find so it is wise to start searching well before you need them so that you will have several options and not be tempted to leap straight into the first one.

4 Most new businesses will find it preferable to rent rather than buy premises initially.

5 Potential premises must be evaluated against a carefully prepared checklist of factors of importance to your business.

6 The one-off costs of occupation as well as the ongoing overheads need to be carefully assessed.

7 Having found suitable premises you should not commit yourself to them until you have ensured that they conform to all the relevant regulations.

8 You will need the help of a solicitor with most business leases as there are many potential pitfalls to avoid.

9 Working from home can be a low cost and low risk way of starting your business, maybe for a trial period, but it is necessary to be aware of all the possible drawbacks.

10 Managed workshops can offer ideal premises for many new businesses and you should check up on their availability in your area.

7 Insurance

Aims of this chapter

- Certain insurance cover, required by law, is explained in the first section
- Additional insurance cover, though not compulsory may still be highly recommended. Other insurance may be of less immediate value. This chapter will compare different types of discretionary insurance
- The final section will explore the best way of buying the insurance you need

Mandatory insurance

1 **Employer's liability.** If you employ any staff at all you must by law take out an employer's liability insurance policy. This would ensure that any employee injured, killed or harmed whilst in your employment would receive proper compensation. For a small firm with very few staff the cost should not exceed £25 per annum.

2 **Vehicle insurance.** All motor vehicles must have third party insurance cover. However, if you plan to use your present vehicle in connection with your new business you will have to change your insurance policy to cover commercial use. If you don't do this you could find yourself without third party insurance cover if you have an accident.

3 **Safety insurance.** It is also a legal requirement that separate insurance cover is taken out for certain types of potentially dangerous plant and equipment including lifting gear and pressure vessels.

Recommended insurance

1 **Property insurance.** If you own property you should insure the buildings against damage or destruction (usually by fire). If you have a mortgage the bank or building society will insist on buildings insurance cover. If you rent premises this insurance would be the landlord's responsibility, but you should beware that he may try to pass the cost on to you.

2 **Contents.** It is essential to insure any contents owned by you inside the building. A business can soon accumulate equipment and

materials worth quite a lot of money. What's more, if these were bought on credit the debt would not be destroyed by fire even if the materials were.

3 Public liability. If your place of work will be visited by members of the public, whether it's customers, salesmen, delivery men or anyone not in your employment they could sue you for damages if they are injured or harmed in any way on your premises. The same would apply to any third parties injured or harmed when working for your business somewhere else, for example, employees working on a site. If you are going to invite customers to your premises you really do need public liability insurance cover. It won't cost much, maybe £25 per annum for a small business.

4 Product liability. If the malfunction of your product would cause harm, injury or loss to other people or businesses it would be wise to take out product liability insurance. For example, if you make life jackets and somebody drowns because it did not inflate you could face a large claim against your business. To take a different example, if you supply a large manufacturer with components and one of your parts is responsible for a failure of the equipment, which the manufacturer then has to put right, he may pass on the cost to you. However, if you make low value, low risk items like pullovers, product liability insurance would probably not be cost effective. You would simply replace any defective goods.

5 Goods in transit. If you will be delivering high value consignments of goods (whether by your own transport or other carriers) it will pay you to have them insured against loss and damage whilst in transit. However, goods in transit policies can be quite expensive so you would have to weigh up the risk relative to the amount of money you can afford to spend on the insurance.

6 Life insurance. If you are married and especially if you have children you need to make arrangements to cover their continued well-being. This is life insurance, but you must distinguish between life insurance as an investment and life insurance to cover your family against a disaster. The latter will cost you much less than the former. You should decide how much your family would need in the event of your death to pay off the mortgage, any other debts, plus maybe a lump sum to provide annual income for your family. The cheapest form of cover is to take out a 'term policy' for a fixed sum for a limited number of years, for example £50,000 cover for five years. You may feel that in five years' time your business will be more established and so you can review your life insurance requirements at that stage. In the meantime a basic term policy could achieve your objective of providing security for your family at the lowest possible cost.

7 Partnership insurance. There are two important reasons why partners, or directors/shareholders of limited companies should take out some kind of insurance cover against the death of one of the partners or directors.

Firstly, the partner who died would own a share of the business. That share of the business, together with all his other assets, would be left in his will to his next of kin or other beneficiaries. It might be his wife, son, brother, friend, in fact anybody. But what if the remaining partner does not want his ex-partner's wife, son, brother or friend as his new partner? In this situation this remaining partner has a real problem unless he has the cash to buy out the share of the new partner. Partnership insurance can be taken out to cover this eventuality. It is basically a life insurance policy which would pay out on the death of one of the partners. The sum assured would have to be high enough to buy out the largest share in the business of any one partner. For partners this may act as an alternative to life insurance.

The second problem which could arise on the death of a partner would be the loss of the expertise of that partner, which may be vital to the success of that business. Replacing that expertise could be very expensive. Therefore some partnerships take out higher insurance cover than they would need for any single partner. The additional money can then be invested in the business to replace the expertise that has been lost.

8 Directors' liability. As mentioned in Chapter 3, the new offence of wrongful trading created by the Insolvency Act of 1985 could make directors personally liable for at least some of the debts of a company under their control which has gone into liquidation. The Institute of Directors has now introduced a personal insurance scheme to protect company directors against claims brought under the Insolvency Act. Details are available from the Institute at:

The Institute of Directors, 116 Pall Mall, London SW1Y 5ED. Tel: 01 839 1233.

9 More cover. There are many additional kinds of insurance policy that you could take out such as health insurance, pension, loss of profits, loss of earnings, and many more. The importance of these policies to you will depend on many factors including age, family circumstances and the amount of insurance you can afford to buy. Many people starting a new small business will prefer to postpone this kind of discretionary insurance for a short time until they are confident that they can afford to pay the premiums.

Mandatory

Employer's liability

Safety

Vehicle

Recommended

Property

Directors' liability

Contents

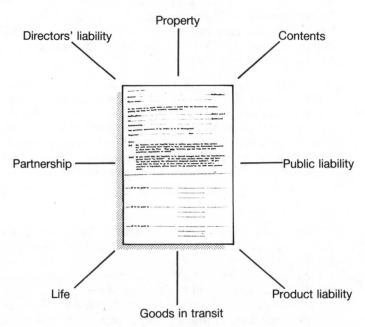

Partnership

Public liability

Life

Product liability

Goods in transit

Fig. 7.1 The main types of insurance

Buying insurance

Most small businesses will require insurance cover in three general areas: life insurance, vehicle insurance, and business insurance.

You would be well advised to contact two or three insurance brokers and ask for quotes for your requirements in those three areas. As a small business it will almost certainly cost you less to have combined business policies to cover your requirements in each of those three general areas.

You should use an insurance broker to help you in two ways. Firstly, he can explain the alternative types of insurance cover available in the general areas you require, and secondly he can shop around for the best value-for-money policies on offer from the insurance companies. An insurance broker does not charge you for those services. He makes his living through earning commission from the insurance companies on the policies he sells.

Fig. 7.2 Banks offer their own insurance services

Ask your professional advisers about good insurance brokers in the area. Try to talk to existing businesses and see what they do about insurance and where they buy their insurance. The main thing is to go and talk to more than one broker, try to assess their level of expertise on business insurance and their genuineness in wanting to help you.

Banks also offer advice on insurance and many high street banks do have their own insurance companies or departments who can arrange cover for you.

There are three important rules about buying insurance cover:

1 **Don't try to cheat!** You must resist the temptation to try to save money by cutting down on the sum insured. If you have under-insured and you need to make a claim, you could lose out significantly.

2 **Understand your insurance.** Make sure you know exactly what your insurance does cover you for. Finding this out through reading the insurance policy is easier said than done. Get your broker to explain exactly what you are covered for and what the policy document means.

3 **Be insured from day one.** That day could be sooner than the date on which you will start trading. For example, it could be the date when you take over your premises and are having equipment or stock delivered.

Summary

1 Employer's liability, vehicle business use and certain kinds of safety insurance are legal requirements for any business.

2 Optional insurance will vary in its importance to each individual, but you will almost certainly want to insure your assets and many businesses will need to have public and/or product liability insurance. It is often said that new businesses should insure initially only against catastrophes: events which, without insurance, would finish off the business. Desirable insurance such as life insurance or a pension scheme have to be postponed until it can be afforded.

3 It is sensible to use an insurance broker to help you to buy insurance and to explain to you exactly what you are, and are not, covered for.

4 Always ensure that you have enough cover in the areas of insurance that you need and that it begins soon enough.

8 Value Added Tax

Aims of this chapter

- To look initially at exactly what VAT is and how it works
- To explain the VAT threshold together with the implications of compulsory registration for many new businesses
- Some new businesses with a low turnover can choose whether or not to register for VAT. This chapter will look at the advantages and disadvantages of doing so
- To explain this procedure for registration

The basic principles of VAT

VAT is designed to tax you on the value added element of your business activities. In other words it taxes you on the difference between the cost of the materials, equipment and services you buy in and the price of the goods or services you sell.

Output tax

Most goods and services which are bought and sold in the UK are liable for VAT. The current rate of VAT is 15 per cent. If your business is registered for VAT it means that you have to add a tax of 15 per cent onto the price that you charge your customer. This is known as an output tax. You would be required to keep records of all your sales and the amount of VAT that you have charged on them. So a typical engineering company might write out an invoice similar to the one shown in fig. 8.1 on the next page.

Every three months you have to add up to the total of your sales and the total VAT that you have added to your invoices over the last three months. You then have to fill in and return a form (called VAT 100) to the Customs and Excise which discloses these figures. You owe to the Customs and Excise the money you have charged in VAT to your customers.

Input tax

However, the authorities will also owe you money because you can claim back any VAT that has been charged on the goods and services that your business has bought. You also keep records of all your purchases, or 'inputs'. At the end of the three month period you add up all the VAT that you have paid out for your purchases. This sum is your input tax. This is money that the Customs and Excise owes to you.

'Value-added' tax

The difference between your output and your input represents the value that your business has added to the product or service. It is on this 'value added' element that you must pay Value Added Tax. Therefore when you make your quarterly return you deduct any input tax that you are owed from the output tax that you owe to the Customs and Excise, and simply send a cheque for the balance. It

---

INVOICE

Invoice to:
Jones Manufacturing Ltd
Riverside Works
New Street
Midshires

Invoice date: 24/9/89
Invoice: 9758

Holmepoint Engineering Ltd
Unit 2
Parkside Industrial Estate
Newtown

VAT Reg. No. 123 4567 89

Qty	Description	Unit price £	Total price £
20	Mild steel collars to spec. 20231	10.00	200.00
10	Pressed steel trays to spec. 64/B	5.00	50.00
	Total goods		250.00
	VAT @ 15%		37.50
	Total amount due		287.50

Fig. 8.1 Record keeping: a sales invoice

---

is possible, as will be seen later in the chapter, that the Customs and Excise could end up owing you money, in which case, you would send the quarterly VAT Return off and the money will be repaid directly into your bank account about a month later.

Record keeping

VAT involves stringent procedures on record keeping. All invoices must be kept and filed in an orderly manner for both sales and purchases. The details of those invoices must also be recorded in an appropriate manner in the firm's books so that you can work out your liability for VAT at the end of every three month period. Firms receive periodic visits from the VAT inspector to check that their record keeping is in order. It it not the purpose of this book to explain how you should manage your business after you have started trading, but you should be aware of the importance of accurate VAT record keeping. It would be wise to consult your accountant and get it right from day one. The Customs and Excise do publish a large number of leaflets dealing with different aspects of VAT. You can request a booklet which lists all these publications, enabling you to select those of relevance to your proposed new business.

Compulsory registration

The VAT threshold

Regulations state that if your turnover has reached a certain level (£23,600 in the tax year 1989-1990), or is expected to reach that level over the next trading year, you must register for VAT. This means that if your business averages a turnover much in excess of £400 per week it has reached the VAT threshold. This is not a very high figure. Unless you are going to have a business where the vast proportion of the costs will be made up of your own time, it is unlikely that you would be able to make a good living out of an annual turnover as low as £23,600. If you anticipate running your business full-time and keeping your turnover below this figure you should check your costings and your budget most carefully to make certain that your projected turnover will be enough. Ask your accountant if he agrees with you.

Unavoidable registration

Some people will be budgeting for a turnover in excess of £23,600 in their first year of trading. In such cases there is no decision to be made. You will have to register for VAT so you might as well get it out of the way at the planning stage before you start trading.

Voluntary registration

Some businesses expect to start very small but to gradually build up their turnover. There may be some delay before turnover is projected to reach the VAT threshold level. If you're in this category you have to decide whether to register for VAT from the outset or whether to put it off until the last possible minute.

The advantages of registering for VAT

1 **Credibility.** This factor will almost certainly apply if you are hoping to sell your product or service to other businesses. They know that if your business is not registered for VAT it must be a very small business. They may then make the assumption that you will be too small to provide them with the kind of service that they require. This conclusion may be totally unfair in your case, but others don't know that. They may have an image of 'back street, fly-by-night' businesses which they associate with unreliable deliveries, dubious quality and sub-standard materials. It may therefore be essential to register your business for VAT before you have to in order to create the right image with your potential customers.

2 **Price competitiveness.** Still assuming that your customers are other businesses, who are themselves registered for VAT, you could be placing youself at a competitive disadvantage when you are giving quotations for jobs if your business is not registered for VAT. It is true that if you are registered you will have to add 15 per cent onto your price, but your trade customers won't notice this because they claim back all the VAT they pay out on their purchases. As far as your business customers are concerned the price they are interested in is the 'ex-VAT' price which is always the one quoted in business to business dealings. If you were to register for VAT you might be able to bring down this 'ex-VAT' price. As a VAT registered business you would be able to claim back the VAT on your business purchases, including your supplies of raw materials or components and many of your overheads such as telephone bills, stationery, vehicle expenses, etc. Most of your competitors are likely to be VAT registered businesses who will be claiming back the VAT element of these costs, so if you were not VAT registered you would effectively be paying more for your supplies than your competitors. It therefore follows that you would have to quote a higher price, and thus risk losing the job, or quote a similar price and thus make less profit.

In some service industries where labour charges form the major part of the business's costs this would be less true because there is obviously no VAT element in your labour costs. The higher your material costs relative to your labour costs the more you stand to save by registering for VAT. But, even for service industries, provided the bulk of your customers are other businesses who can recover the VAT on their purchases, rather than individuals who cannot, you should be more competitive on price if you are registered for VAT.

3 Suppliers. It may be your suppliers rather than your customers who force you to register for VAT. Many 'trade only' warehouses or cash and carry stores deal only with other businesses. Quite a number of these suppliers use the VAT number as evidence of the fact that people wanting to buy from them are *'bona fide'* businesses. Some are very strict about this and may refuse to supply you at all if you do not have a VAT number. Others are less strict and may take a copy of your business letterheading as sufficient proof that you are in business. However, you also need to make sure that the absence of a VAT number would not lead to your getting less of a discount from the supplier.

4 Initial investment. If you will be investing a reasonable sum in supplies and/or equipment when you start your business you could be laying out quite a lot of money for VAT on these items. For every £1000 you spend, £130 will be VAT (assuming that the goods are liable for VAT @ 15 per cent). If you register your business before you start trading you would be able to recoup all this VAT at the end of your first three months of trading. This could be very beneficial to your cash flow. It is possible to claim back VAT on purchases for the six months prior to registration, but it would involve quite a lot of administrative work and would be less beneficial to your cash flow.

5 VAT profit makers. Some businesses may benefit by registering for VAT. If you sell goods or services which are zero-rated for VAT you will not be adding VAT onto your customers' bills so you will not owe the Customs and Excise any output tax at the end of each quarter. The chances are that many of the supplies which you buy in will also be zero-rated, but many of your overhead costs such as telephone, vehicle expenses, advertising, etc, will include VAT @ 15 per cent. On these costs you would be able to recover £130 for every £1000 you spent if you were registered for VAT. You would therefore be in the position of receiving a refund from the Customs and Excise every three months.

The range of zero-rated items has been whittled away somewhat by successive budgets, but a rough guide to the areas of business which are still zero-rated follows. This is not a comprehensive list, but if you think that your product or service could be zero-rated you should contact your local VAT office and ask for confirmation.

It is also worth noting that the harmonization of taxes across the European Community which could result from the creation of the Single European Market could affect British VAT rates significantly over the next few years.

Zero-rated outputs include:

a Food (excluding hot food). You can probably still remember the outcry that followed the imposition of VAT on fish and chips following the 1984 budget!

b Books

c Fuel (excluding any road fuel).

d New buildings. This is an extremely complex area of regulation where guidance from your local VAT office is essential, but broadly speaking the construction of new buildings is a zero-rated activity but any work on existing buildings such as repairs, maintenance, conversion, or enlargement, is liable to VAT @ 15 per cent.

e Residential caravans and houseboats. This category includes services provided in connection with these items but excludes holiday accommodation.

f Drugs and medical suppliers and equipment.

g Protective boots and helmets.

h Children's clothing and footwear.

Exempt supplies

Before examining the disadvantages of registering for VAT it is important to discuss the meaning of the term 'exempt outputs' in order to clear up any confusion with 'zero-rated outputs'. Whereas zero-rated goods or services do in theory have VAT added (but since it is at a percentage rate of zero it makes no difference) exempt supplies are exactly that: exempt from VAT, outside the system. This means that businesses dealing totally in exempt supplies can't be registered for VAT and will not be able to claim back the VAT element of their business purchases. Businesses which deal partly in exempt goods and partly in taxable goods will be able to negotiate a proportion of their input tax which they can reclaim.

Exempt goods and services include:

a Land. The sale and rental of land and buildings are classed as exempt but this category excludes 'holiday' rents such as camping sites or holiday flats.

b Insurance.

c Betting.

d Finance. This includes businesses which deal in money, such as finance houses and stockbrokers, but excludes financial services like accountancy, debt collection, and consultancy.

e Education. This includes any non-profit making organizations in the public or private sector, but the income of any profit seeking businesses involved in nursery education, schools, business training, and so on would be liable for VAT @ 15 per cent.

f Health. This covers the services of registered practitioners like doctors, dentists and opticians.

g Burial and cremation.

h Sports competitions.

This list is again meant only as an introductory guide and does not pretend to be comprehensive. If you think that all or part of your sales may involve exempt supplies you should check on the exact position with your local Customs and Excise office.

The disadvantages of registering for VAT

Some businesses are not going to gain anything by registering for VAT any sooner than they have to. It will be in their interest to delay registration for as long as possible. There now follow some typical examples of the sorts of businesses which would probably be better off remaining outside the VAT system.

'Farmhouse Furnishing'

Bill has a one man business producing traditional high quality hand made furniture. He has no desire to expand his business, preferring not to employ staff. Bill's workshop is in an old barn next to his house so his overheads are very low, his own time forming by far the largest part of his costs. He is therefore quite satisfied by the living he can earn from a turnover of around £20,000 per annum. There are a number of reasons why it would not pay him to register for VAT.

a Price. If Bill were VAT registered he would have to add 15 per cent onto his selling prices. The bulk of his customers are individuals who would not be able to recover that VAT. Bill's furniture is already expensive. A typical dining table and chairs is already sold at £2000, so with VAT added, the price would go up to £2300. Bill thinks that this extra 15 per cent would put off some of his customers.

b Administration. Bill is adamant that he did not start a business in order to spend his time doing paperwork. Bill wanted his own business so that he could spend his time making furniture. Although the book-keeping for VAT is not as onerous as people sometimes make it out to be it is very wise for Bill as a one man business to keep his administrative burden to the minimum so that he can use his own time as profitably as possible.

c Input Tax. It is true that if Bill were registered for VAT he could claim back the VAT element in his purchases. However, timber represents a relatively small proportion of the cost of Bill's furniture, his own labour amounting to the largest part of the cost. Being registered for VAT would therefore offer very little advantage in terms of a reduction in costs.

All in all therefore, Bill has very little incentive to register for VAT. The same principle would apply if he were a potter, a painter, a boat builder, or a vintage car restorer. If something is made in a very labour intensive way and is sold directly to the public, registering for VAT earlier than needs be is unlikely to be in the business owner's best interests.

'Rapid Repairs'

Alan is 28, and gave up his job as a service engineer with a large electrical retailer in order to start his own business. He offers a general repair service for household electrical goods in his local area. Needing only a desk and a telephone point for his business premises he is able to run the business from home. All the repair work is carried out on the spot in the customer's home. Alan knows the business inside out and is well aware that with lower overheads he can be very competitive on price compared to the larger companies and he is sure that he can provide an equally good service. His customers are all individuals who could not recover the VAT that Alan would have to add on to his bills. Alan realises that in the long run if he is going to succeed in expanding his business he will have to be able to compete effectively and charge VAT to his customers. Initially however, his attractive prices with no VAT will help him to build up a good customer base, and as his business becomes more established and better known he should be able to raise his prices.

Alan has a lot in common with many small service businesses such as plumbers, electricians, window cleaners, decorators and gardeners who view the domestic market as their main source of trade. The price advantage will probably be a big help in attracting customers while they are trying to get their business established.

'Ocean View Guest House'

Bob has bought a small guest house in Cornwall. It has nine letting bedrooms and running it will be a full-time job for Bob and his wife during the summer season. Bob's costs fall into three main categories:

a Food. This is the largest item of expenditure but since it is zero-rated for VAT Bob would gain no cost advantage here if he did register.

b Overheads. The greater proportion of Bob's overheads would be exempt or zero-rated items such as his mortgage repayments, rates, heat and light, insurance, postage, etc. A small proportion of his overheads: telephone, stationery, decorating and vehicle expenses for example, would include reclaimable input tax but this would not amount to very much money each year so it would not reduce his costs by very much.

c Labour. Labour is a considerable cost, and whether it covers the time of Bob, his wife or that of his hired staff there is no cost reduction to be gained here from being registered for VAT.

Bob quite rightly concluded that his costs would hardly be reduced at all if he were VAT registered but he would have to add 15 per cent on to his prices. In a very price competitive business where a lot of guest houses are not VAT registered adding this premium onto his prices could be a severe disadvantage. An £80 per week bed, breakfast and evening meal package would become £92 if VAT had to be added, a very big increase when there are so many non-VAT registered guest houses to choose from. It is in Bob's interests to avoid VAT at all costs. With nine bedrooms he couldn't increase his turnover much above £23,600 even if he wanted to. Rather than go over the VAT threshold it would even pay him to finish his season a couple of weeks earlier than he planned.

Early registration

Even if you are certain that it is not in your interest to register for VAT, it may still not be to your advantage to delay registration if you know that your turnover will reach the VAT threshold in a fairly short time. If you register after six months or one year of trading for example, you will have to make a number of changes which would have been better accomodated from the outset, such as:

a Book-keeping. You may have to change your method of book-keeping in order to conform to the requirements of Customs and Excise.

b Stationery. Once you are registered your VAT number would have to be displayed on all your stationery including invoices, statements, etc. If you have already had supplies printed it would be costly to overprint everything with your VAT number, and any do-it-yourself method of adding it would look scruffy and unprofessional.

c Costings. You would have to recalculate all your costings to take account of reclaiming your input tax.

d Price lists. You may have to reprint price lists, publicity material or terms of business forms.

How to register for VAT

Things you need

The first step is to contact your local VAT office. You will find them in the telephone directory under 'Customs and Excise'. You should ring them up and ask them for two, or in the case of partnerships, three things:

1 **Explanatory booklet.** The VAT office has a basic booklet which outlines the procedures for registering for VAT. It will probably not tell you much more than you already know from reading this chapter, but will be up-to-date and will include any recent changes which may have occurred since the publication of this book.

2 **Form VAT 1.** This form is called 'Notification of Liability to be Registered for Value Added Tax' and is the form you fill in to become VAT registered. The next section shows how to fill this form in.

3 **Form VAT 2 (for partnerships only).** This is simply a form for filling in the names and addresses of all the partners in a partnership. A limited company does not need to fill in this form even if there are several directors and/or shareholders because it is the company and not the individual directors or shareholders that is considered to be the VAT registered 'person'.

Filling in form VAT 1

You can see a VAT 1 form completed in the name of a fictitious business in fig. 8.2 (pages 126-7). It is not difficult to fill in. However, it would be a good idea to have a list of queries to ask the Customs and Excise when you telephone for your VAT 1 form. There are a couple of points to make about this form.

1 **Business classification.** Notice that point 5 (near the bottom of the first page) asks you to enter the trade classification of your business, which is something that you are unlikely to know. If you give a few brief details about the nature of your busniess the official from the VAT office will soon tell you your trade classification. Alternatively, you can ask for the trade classification leaflet (VAT 41) and choose the most appropriate one for yourself.

2 **Rate of VAT.** If you are not certain whether some of your sales will be taxable at the standard rate, the zero-rate, or may be

exempt, you should also check this with the VAT office. You will then be able to fill in section 10 as accurately as possible. Of course, you will not be in any way bound by any figures you put in sections 10 or 12, they are for guidance only.

Filling in the rest of form VAT 1 is quite straightforward.

Filling in form VAT 2: partnerships

A form VAT 2 must accompany your VAT 1 if you are a partnership and wish to register for VAT. As can be seen from fig. 8.3 (page 128) it is very simple to fill in, requiring no more than the name, home address and signature of each partner.

Special schemes for retailers

There are no fewer than nine special VAT schemes for retailers. The word 'retailer' in this case does not just refer to shopkeepers but is used to cover any business selling goods or services directly to the public where it is impractical to issue a separate tax invoice for each individual transaction. The special schemes for retailers use your gross daily takings and your purchases of supplies or stocks as the basis for calculating the output tax you owe. As you can imagine, with nine different schemes it is a very complex matter choosing the most suitable one. Certain types of retailing operations can save quite a lot of money by opting for the correct scheme. It is therefore vital to have an accountant who understands your kind of business and can advise you on the best retail scheme.

Summary

1 Many new businesses have to register for VAT from the outset because they know that their turnover will be well in excess of an annual rate of £23,600.

2 For businesses with a lower turnover registration will be voluntary. Those who will mainly serve business customers would normally find it advantageous to register, whilst those selling mainly to individuals, who are not in a position to reclaim the VAT, will usually be well advised to avoid VAT if possible. However, any business which expects to exceed the VAT threshold fairly quickly will find it more efficient to register from the outset.

3 For most businesses, registering for VAT is a simple procedure involving the completion of only one form. Any queries can be dealt with over the telephone by the Customs and Excise. Retailers or businesses with a significant proportion of exempt items in their turnover face a more complex decision and should consult professional advisers if in doubt.

Fig. 8.2 An example of form VAT 1

VALUE ADDED TAX
Application for Registration

HM Customs and Excise

You should open up this form and read the notes before you answer these questions. Please write clearly in ink.

For official use

Date of receipt	
Local office code and registration number	
Name	
Trade name	
Taxable turnover	

Applicant and business

1 Full name

JPD MARKETING SERVICES LIMITED

2 Trading name

3 Address

10 GEORGE STREET
ALDERLEY EDGE
CHESHIRE

Phone no.
0625-582181

Postcode SK9 7EJ

4 Status of business

Limited company ✓ Company incorporation certificate no. 2242330 and date 08 04 19 89

Sole proprietor ☐ Partnership ☐ Other-specify

5 Business activity
BUSINESS CONSULTANTS

Trade classification 8 6 5 5

6 Computer user ☐

Repayments of VAT

7 ☐ Bank sorting code and account no. 12 34 56 98765432

National Girobank account no.

VAT 1   please continue overleaf ——→

126

Compulsory registrations

8 Date of first taxable supply | day `30` | month `06` | year `1989`   Value of taxable supplies in the 12 months from that date. £ `40,000`

9 Date from which you have to be registered   day `30` month `06` year `1989`

10 Exemption from compulsory registration ☐

     expected value of zero-rated supplies in the next 12 months   £ ☐

Other types of registration

11 Taxable supplies below registration limits ☐

     value of taxable supplies in the last 12 months   £ ☐

12 No taxable supplies made yet ☐

     (a) expected annual value of taxable supplies   £ ☐

     (b) expected date of first taxable supply   day month year `19`

Business changes and transfers

13 Business transferred as a going concern ☐

     (a) date of transfer or change of legal status   day month year `19`

     (b) name of previous owner

     (c) previous VAT registration number (if known)

14 Transfer of VAT registration number ☐

Related businesses

15 Other VAT registrations   Yes ☑   No ☐

Declaration – You must complete this declaration.

16 I *JOHN HUME*

(Full name in BLOCK LETTERS)

declare that all the entered details and information in any accompanying documents are correct and complete.

Signature *JHum.*   Date `30/6/89`

Proprietor ☐   Partner ☐   Director ☑   Company Secretary ☐   Authorised Official ☐   Trustee ☐

For official use

Registration	Obligatory	Exemption	Voluntary	Intending	Transfer of Regn. no.
Approved — Initial/Date					
Refused — Initial/Date					
Form Issued — Initial/Date	VAT 9/ Other	VAT 8	VAT 7	Letter	Approval Letter

VAT 1 F3733(APRIL 1988)

Printed in the U.K. for H.M.S.O. 3/88 Dd.812/0617 C.12500 9889 I.16/5

127

Fig. 8.3 An example of form VAT 2

Crown copyright. Reproduced with permission of Controller of HMSO

Value Added Tax	For official use

Notification Of Liability To Be Registered For Value Added Tax

Registration number

If the notification on Form VAT 1 is for a partnership, please list below, in BLOCK LETTERS, the full names of all the partners and their addresses.

This form must be signed by each partner in the space provided and forwarded together with Form VAT 1 to the Customs and Excise VAT office.

Any changes in the composition of the partnership must be notified to your local VAT office immediately.

Full name *ALAN SMITH*
Address including postode *I LONDON ROAD*
ANYTOWN AY2 1BS

Signature *ASmith* Date *29/9/89*

Full name *JILL BROWN*
Address including postode *19 CHURCH ST*
ANYTOWN AY1 1RT

Signature *JBrown* Date *29/9/89*

Full name
Address including postode

Signature .... Date ....

Full name
Address including postode

Signature .... Date ....

Full name
Address including postode

Signature .... Date ....

VAT 2   F 3736 (1980)

9 Employing others

Aims of this chapter

- The initial decision to employ staff will be examined and possible alternative measures outlined
- Methods of recruiting staff will be discussed
- Employment regulations will be outlined

The decision to employ staff

Sooner or later most new businesses will expand to the size where they need to employ others. But this is a big decision. It increases your administration, your weekly overheads and the demands on your managerial abilities. For these reasons many new businesses will rightly decide to concentrate on other aspects of starting their business and will think about employing staff only after they have succeeded in getting the business moving. In the short term, however, there may be alternatives to employing staff which would give you the extra help you need.

1 Family and friends. While you are still setting up the business you will invariably receive a vast amount of help not just from your family but also from well-meaning friends.

2 Freelance staff. Some employment needs are well catered for by freelance people who work for themselves and give you a bill for their services. Many jobs could be covered in this way including salesmen, delivery men, cleaners, secretaries, book-keepers, and so on. It may be more expensive on an hourly basis but reduces your overheads and administration and if your staffing needs are still somewhat irregular this method would be particularly appropriate.

3 Outworkers. Self-employed outworkers are very common in some trades. If your product (or parts of it) could be made or assembled by people working at home outworkers could be a very useful alternative to employing staff, especially in the early days.

4 Sub-contract. A similar alternative is to sub-contract part of your workload when you can't cope. You will avoid being stuck with permanent staff if the workload then drops.

5 Part-time staff. When you do need your first employees it may be possible to employ part-time staff. If their earnings fall below the tax and National Insurance threshold your administration would be greatly reduced.

6 Government schemes. Schemes for the unemployed can be a low cost way of employing staff either permanently or for short projects. You can often get high level staff such as graduates or managers and of course you can employ youngsters under the YTS, which may offer the new business an ideal way of recruiting and training its first employee. More details of all such schemes can be obtained from the Training Agency.

Recruiting staff

1 Advertising. The difficulty and cost of generating enough suitable applications for any job will differ around the country depending on the local unemployment level. In some areas, for all but the highest level jobs, your first call should certainly be to the local Jobcentre or careers office. Your local technical college may also be a useful source of recruits. It would be worth making enquiries to identify the nearest college which runs courses specializing in your type of work. Only if these options fail to produce satisfactory results should you spend money on advertising.

2 The job description. However you advertise your job it is crucial to incorporate a detailed and accurate job description otherwise you will receive many unsuitable applications. A job description should cover a thorough explanation of the duties which the successful applicant would be expected to carry out, any qualifications or experience which all applicants should have, the salary, any additional benefits and the hours of work. Any special requirements, such as willingness to work away from home or knowledge of foreign languages, should also be mentioned. A good test of the ability of your job description is to ask a couple of friends to read it through and give you their understanding of the job. If it's misleading then you can make the necessary amendments.

3 Processing the applications. The more comprehensive your job description the easier it will be for you to assess the suitability of written applications. You don't want to waste time interviewing any applicants who would be unsuitable.

4 Interviews. Four candidates is enough for most small businesses to interview. An initial group session to explain about the job and the company to all candidates will save time and will help to place them at their ease. Interviews are a two-way process. You are also being assessed. For most jobs it won't just be qualifications that

Jogger's World

SALES ASSISTANT

- Interested in retail sportsgoods?
- Well educated and keen to learn?
- Friendly personality and good appearance?
- Aged 18-21?

YES?

Then we'd like to hear from you. This position includes dealing with customers and enquiries, working on the checkout desk, stocktaking and ordering, and general administrative duties.

We are offering competitive rates plus incentives, excellent prospects, and a friendly, busy working environment.

For full job description and an
application form write to:

THE MANAGER, JOGGER'S WORLD,
15 HIGH STREET, SMALLTOWN,
WESSEX, SM1 2XT.

Fig. 9.1 Recruiting your staff

matter but how well the individual would fit into your business, and, importantly, how well you could get on with him, or her.

Regulations

 There are some important regulations to observe when you do employ staff.

1 Contract of employment. Within 13 weeks of the job commencing you are legally obliged to provide the employee with a contract of employment. Blank contract of employment forms can be purchased from a business stationer already printed with all the information which must be covered by the contract.

2 Itemized pay statement. You must, by law, provide all employees with an itemized pay statement. Pads of blank pay statements are also available from the business stationer, as are small sealable 'pay packet' envelopes.

3 Tax and National Insurance. You are required by law to deduct income tax and National Insurance contributions from your employees at source before you pay them. The inland revenue have strict procedures for doing this and provide tables explaining exactly how much to deduct each week for different rates of pay. Once you have understood the procedures they are really very simple to follow, but they may not appear so at first sight. Therefore it is worthwhile getting your local tax office to show you exactly how to make the deductions and fill in the appropriate forms.

4 Employee's rights. There are many laws protecting the employee's rights to redundancy pay, maternity leave, to healthy and safe working conditions, against unfair dismissal, etc. They all vary according to the employee's length of service and hours of work, but even part-time employees who do not necessarily pay tax or National Insurance can still qualify for these rights. Taking on staff of any kind can therefore represent an extensive commitment and all regulations should be thoroughly investigated beforehand.

5 Employment agencies. If you are going to use your staff to work for your customers on their premises you will need a licence from the Department of Employment. This does not just apply to obvious employment agencies, such as secretarial bureaux, but to any sub-contracting of staff, even if your customer actually pays their wages whilst they are working for him. It would therefore apply to a business supplying contract cleaning staff, catering staff, domestic cleaners or nannies, or to industrial service staff such as welders, maintenance engineers or computer programmers if they were hired out to work for other companies.

Summary

1 Most new businesses are unlikely to need to employ staff before they have started trading.

2 As an initial step alternatives to employing staff, such as using outworkers, should be investigated.

3 If you do decide to employ staff you must manage the recruitment process very carefully. Recruiting the right staff is very time-consuming but recruiting the wrong staff can be very expensive.

4 Before you begin to recruit any staff you should ensure that you fully understand all the legal obligations you must fulfill as employer.

10 Marketing for the new business

Aims of this chapter

This chapter will examine:

- How marketing is a much broader management function than simply selling or promoting the business
- The difference between inward looking and outward looking businesses
- The importance of developing an intimate knowledge and understanding of customers
- Targeting and specialization
- The marketing mix and the way it should be managed to achieve customer satisfaction

What is marketing?

Marketing is not just selling

Marketing is not just advertising

Marketing is not just market research

Marketing is not just good design

Marketing is not just quality

But, marketing is **all** these things, and many more.

There are some very complex definitions of the word 'marketing' but a very simple one is as follows:

Marketing is about winning and keeping customers and making a profit out of doing so.

In this definition can be found the two things that will be more important than anything else to your business – *customers* and *profits*.

Good marketing is outward looking

It is often easier to understand the meaning and importance of marketing if you put yourself in the position of a customer rather than a business owner. As individuals we are all customers for many different products and services. We all know when we feel satisfied with a product and would buy it again from the same company. We also know the feeling when we feel really dissatisfied, even cheated, over a purchase and would not take our custom back to that manufacturer or retailer at any price.

Giving the customer what he wants

As the customer, if we get what we want then we are happy with the purchase. 'Getting what we want' embraces many things including quality, reliability, delivery time, price, styling, performance, service, and cleanliness to name but a few.

'Getting what we want' will vary, depending on the product or service we are buying. For most purchases we will have a conscious or sub-conscious list of attributes that we are expecting when we make the purchase. If we get all the benefits we are expecting then we will be happy, satisfied customers. If some of those expected benefits don't materialize when we use or consume the product, we will be disappointed, dissatisfied customers.

What exactly is the list of benefits that customers of your product or service will be looking for when they make the decision to purchase? If you can come up with this list then your objective as a business owner is crystal clear. Your aim is to organize your business to provide its customers with the full range of benefits on that list. If your business provides more of those benefits than your competitors, then your business is the one which will come out on top in the market.

Marketing is a continuous process which begins at the research and planning stage and extends well beyond the point of sale. The interest your business shows in its customers after they have parted with their money could be the crucial factor in deciding whether they (and all their friends and acquaintances) bring their custom back to you or take it to one of your competitors in future. If you want to win and keep satisfied customers everything in your business must be geared to 'giving the customer what he wants'.

'Marketing is not just selling'

It is vitally important for all business owners to understand the difference between marketing and selling. There are only two basic elements in the selling process, firstly having something to sell, and secondly persuading the customer to buy it. This is an inward looking activity where the emphasis is on the seller wanting to sell the items for sale rather than on the customers wanting to buy them. This has given rise to a lot of suspicion about the selling process and resentment towards salesmen, who are often cast in the part of the worst kind of second hand car salesman, or door-to-door encyclopaedia salesman.

Marketing is not just selling! Marketing turns the selling process onto its head, looks outward and puts itself into the customer's shoes. Instead of producing goods and then persuading people to buy them, the marketing oriented company first of all finds out what consumers want to buy, then designs, produces and makes available a suitable product (or service). All the emphasis is outward looking. When it comes to selling the product, activities such as informing consumers about the product and making it easy and convenient to purchase become much more important than the hard sell. The act of making a sale becomes the end result of a carefully planned and effectively carried out marketing strategy. The objective of this marketing strategy is to use all the resources and strengths of the business to meet the needs of customers in its market in a way which is profitable to the business.

Marketing myopia

Some small business owners are inclined to be in love with their product. They have thought it up, designed it, developed it and they think it's wonderful! This can be very, very dangerous. If you're not careful you will become inward looking and self-centred thinking more highly of your own darling product than the needs of your customers. Your potential customers on the other hand care only about their needs and if your business does not supply a product which meets those needs they will not buy from you. The only reason your company exists is to satisfy the needs of customers. If it fails to do that it will not continue to exist because it won't have enough sales. The danger of being inward looking and product oriented is that you become so wrapped up in your own product that you lose sight of the real needs of your customers. This is known as marketing myopia. It is a very apt name because it is very short-sighted to put your own ideas or priorities before the needs and priorities of your customers. Marketing is an outward looking process that puts the customers' needs at the centre of all the plans and actions of the business.

Ask yourself the question 'what business do I hope to be in'? How would you answer this? Some might give the kind of answers shown below:

'I will be in the boat manufacturing business'

'I will be in the business of repairing cars'

'I will be in the replacement window business'

'I will be in the hairdressing business'

Are these answers inward looking or outward looking? For example, the person who is going into business to manufacture boats is in danger of developing marketing myopia if he's not careful. He'll become inward looking, spending all his time designing and producing his idea of the world's best boat with little or no thought as to whether it meets the needs of potential customers. It will then come as a real shock if the new boat doesn't sell well.

It would have been better if the replies had been something like this:

'I will be in the business of helping people to enjoy their leisure time on the water'

'I will be in the business of minimizing the inconvenience suffered by people needing car repairs'

'I will be in the business of helping people to make their home a better place to live in'

'I will be in the business of helping people to look beautiful'

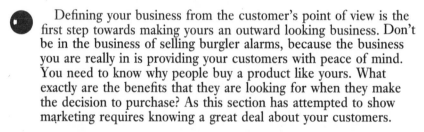 Defining your business from the customer's point of view is the first step towards making yours an outward looking business. Don't be in the business of selling burgler alarms, because the business you are really in is providing your customers with peace of mind. You need to know why people buy a product like yours. What exactly are the benefits that they are looking for when they make the decision to purchase? As this section has attempted to show marketing requires knowing a great deal about your customers.

Knowing your customers

If you're going to be successful at meeting the needs of your customers you will need to know them very well indeed. You need to know who they are, what they are like, why they buy products like yours, what they use them for, where they buy them and how often they purchase. All this information enables you to build up a kind of identikit profile of a typical buyer, which will help you to understand your customers, which, in turn, will help you to organize all aspects of your business to meet the needs of your customers.

The sections that follow contain a number of questions about your customers. See how many you can answer. It is obviously much easier for somebody in an existing business to answer these questions than it is for somebody who has not yet started trading, but, as stressed in Chapter 2, you are supposed to have a very good knowledge of the market you are going to enter, so now put this to the test. See how many you can answer, and in how much detail.

1 Who are your customers?

Sex

1 Are they exclusively male or female?

2 Do they include males and females, and if so, in what proportions?

Age

1 What is the age range of your customers?

2 If the range is wide, which age group(s) provide most customers?

Family status

1 Are your customers mainly single or married?

2 Do they have children?

3 Do they have young or older children?

4 Are they retired?

Income

1 Would you classify the bulk of your customers as:
   a wealthy
   b middle income
   c not very well off?

2 How much disposable income will your customers have for your type of product after they have met their more important financial commitments? For example, it is generally accepted that married couples without children or with grown up children have more disposable income than families with children.

Lifestyle

1 Will your customers be 'stay-at-home' types?

2 Will your customers go out a lot?

3 Will your customers be sporty types?

4 Are your customers likely to be associated with any particular social grouping which is likely to influence their behaviour? Membership of clubs or less formal groups, such as occupational groups, can affect buyers' behaviour, especially with conspicuous items, where their choice may be affected by their desire to 'fit in' with other people in that group.

2 Who are your industrial customers?

If your customers are other businesses rather than individuals there are these different questions that you should be able to answer.

1 Will your customers be large companies or small companies?

2 If a mixture, what proportion will be large, medium and small?

3 If you expect much of your custom to come from large companies, do you know which individuals within those companies will be responsible for their company's decision to place an order with your business?

4 Are your customers likely to belong to any trade association and if so which ones?

3 What do your customers buy?

1 Do your customers buy top of the range or bargain basement products?

2 How much relative importance do your customers attach to product or service features such as performance, reliablity, styling, colour, price, safety, convenience, after sales service, technical back-up, or any other features?

4 Why do your customers buy?

The following questions are very important but are often overlooked by many businesses. They are designed to uncover the real benefits that a customer is hoping to gain as a result of purchasing the product or service.

1 Will your customers buy your product to satisfy a basic everyday need?

2 Will your product be bought as a treat, a luxury, or a gift?

3 Will your customers be trying to solve an emergency problem when they buy from you?

4 Will your customers be buying a leisure or special interest product?

5 Will your customers be making a conspicuous purchase which may be meeting their need to display affluence, style or conformity with a particular social group?

6 What exactly will customers use your product for (or how exactly will they consume it)? It's not always bought for the same purpose as the manufacturers think.

If customers will be other businesses some of the following questions may be more relevant in this category.

1 Will the purchases of your product or service be a very low level decision within the buying company, for example, the ordering of supplies for the toilets?

2 Will it be a vital purchase: a new computer system, or a small and relatively cheap component whose reliable operation in your customer's finished product is of critical importance?

3 Could it come into the category of a conspicuous purchase, such as office furniture?

4 Does it fall into the category of health and safety, or some other product or service which the customer is compelled through legislation, to buy?

5 Is it a product or service which is not considered to be essential to customers and may therefore be one of the first to be given up in hard times?

6 Do you know exactly what your product will be used for?

5 How often do your customers buy?

1 Is it a very infrequent purchase, such as a one-off or once every 10 to 20 years?

2 Is it an infrequent but regular purchase, such as once every two years?

3 Is it a frequent and regular purchase?

4 Is it a frequent but irregular (possibly impulse) purchase?

6 Where do your customers buy?

1 Will many of your customers be grouped in a certain definable geographical area or will they be scattered far and wide?

2 Will customers visit your premises to purchase, or will you visit their premises or home?

3 Is convenience of purchase very important to the customer?

4 Do customers make a shopping trip, for example, to the town centre, in order to buy?

5 Is the purchase process itself a leisure activity for customers: visiting a garden centre, for example?

6 Is the product something that the customer enjoys shopping around for, comparing different products and prices?

7 When do your customers buy?

1 Is trade regular throughout the year?

2 Is trade clearly seasonal and if so, what are the peaks and troughs?

3 Is trade very dependent on a good economic climate?

Targeting customers

The answers to the questions you have just completed plus the market research you undertook in Chapter 2 should have enabled you to build up a profile of the type of customer (business or individual) that you envisage as the most likely buyer of your product or service. This profile becomes your **target customer** and a collection of these people or businesses will be your **target market**. If your marketing is going to be successful, your whole business must be dedicated to meeting the needs and preferences of customers in that target market.

Accurate targeting is vital for the success of a small business. It is unrealistic to think that a small new business can compete directly with the larger, longer established, better known competition. To take business from them the small new business has to be different in some way and this means targeting a small group of customers whose needs are not being very well met by larger competitors. In other words, you have to specialize. You have to do a very narrow range of activities extremely well. The first five winners of the annual Industrial Achievement Award for small businesses all displayed this ability to specialize and to target a precise area of need in the market:

VDU Installations, the first winners, spotted and exploited a need to provide specialized cabling services for companies wishing to network computers. Started on a dining room table in 1977, VDU Installations employed 100 people in 1985.

Microvitec has concentrated on the manufacture of colour monitors. Founder Tony Martinez had realized that the growing sales of home computers (almost invariably without a monitor since they were usually plugged into the television for this purpose) was creating a need for this specialist product. Registered in 1979, Microvitec employed 350 people and turned over £30 million by 1985.

Norfrost, a Scottish manufacturer of freezers now employing over 100 people was the third winner of the award and can date its success to a decision taken in 1977 to stop trying to market a wide range of freezers but to concentrate instead on one model: a small, low cost chest freezer.

Denford Machines Tools, winners of the award in 1984, was an old family firm, struggling after the oil crisis of 1973 but which underwent a dramatic recovery based on targeting the market for small machine tools used for educational and training purposes.

Industrial Clothing Services, the fifth winner, owes its success to offering a cleaning service which no one else had thought of. Motor manufacturers used to regard protective gloves as disposible. Industrial Clothing Services offered to clean and repair them. Ford alone was able to save over £1 million a year as a result.

All these companies succeeded through precise targeting. They identified a clear need amongst a definable group of customer and concentrated on offering a specialist product or service to meet that need. All five success stories are told in much greater detail in *Winners*, R. Bruce, Sidgwick and Jackson Ltd, 1986.

As you will see when you look at the exercise in Chapter 13, it is vital to know this sort of information about your customers if you are going to prepare an effective business plan. The marketing element of that business plan will be dependent upon a close knowledge of your target market and a clear idea of the needs, priorities and preferences of potential customers. It is up to you to respond to these needs. If you can plan and deliver a marketing package which meets customer needs more closely than any of your competitors, you are bound to be successful in the long run.

Marketing mix

Marketing is not just a single monolithic notion, but a blend of ideas, a whole range of benefits, which your business can offer to potential customers. Because there are a number of different aspects of marketing management which must all be combined in a complementary and effective way, the term **'marketing mix'** has

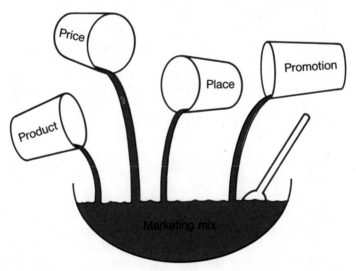

Fig. 10.1 The marketing mix

been coined to describe the different functions which your marketing plan must cover. The marketing mix is made up of four elements and is sometimes referred to as 'the 4 Ps': Product, Price, Place, Promotion.

It is important to look at each of the 4 Ps in turn and consider the kind of marketing decisions which you should be making for each.

Product decisions

A product is not necessarily a physical object which has been manufactured by your business. Your 'product' is whatever you will be selling to customers. A product is 'a package of benefits' designed to meet the needs of your customers. Your 'product' might be a service, like a hairdressing service or a taxi service. Some marketing textbooks use the word 'offering' instead of product because the product is what your business is offering to customers to satisfy their needs.

There is a tendency for new businesses to overvalue the importance of the product, often because the owner-manager is more interested in the product than in other aspects of managing his business. Very often people start a business because they have a particular skill to apply or because they had a good idea about how to make a certain product, or just because they enjoy making it. Of course, the product is very important, but it is not any more important than the other aspects of the marketing mix. They are all important. So don't go overboard and think that because you have a well designed and beautifully manufactured product that it will sell itself. It won't. All the parts of the marketing mix have to be carefully planned to ensure that your business meets all the needs of target customers.

Even the product itself should not just be seen as one single entity. There are a number of aspects of product management, each one of which may have a different, and vital, role to play in satisfying the requirements of your customers.

Your product is a combination of:

1 Specification.
2 Quality.
3 Style.
4 Packaging.
5 Service.

1 **Specification.** In some industries the nature of the product will be completely dictated by the customer who will lay down a strict specification when the order is placed. This should be seen as a good thing. It avoids misunderstanding and it ensures that the

product meets the needs of the customer. However, many new businesses will find themselves in the position of determining their own specifications, so they have to decide on the product 'spec' which will most closely meet the needs of typical customers in the target market. This will involve a number of different decisions.

Product *performance* is often a crucial issue for many new business owners. Many small businesses see the performance of their product as all important. They regard it as a challenge, a matter of pride, to come up with a product which out performs all of its rivals. This may be justifiable in certain markets, for example, the marketing of sports equipment to dedicated competitors. However, the achievement of such high levels of performance has servere cost implications and it will usually be only a very small percentage of the market which is prepared to pay the true cost of top performance specifications. In most markets top performance specifications are not necessary. Adequate performance is all that is required. As long as adequate performance is provided the customer's purchase is likely to be much more strongly influenced by different product features and by the other elements of the marketing mix.

Safety is a fundamental aspect of design. Minimum safety standards are non-negotiable. However, it is interesting to note that there is usually little demand for levels of safety which are higher than the generally accepted minimum standards. There will be exceptions with some safety conscious customers: some people buy Volvo cars for their safety; but normally such customers will form only a small niche in a much larger market. If in any doubt about safety, you should contact your local Trading Standards Office for advice.

2 Quality. There are two dangers for the small businessman on the issue of quality: making it too high or making it too low. A considerable number of small new businesses pay the penalty for falling short on quality. Due to lack of experience, often due to lack of accurate costing, sometimes due to inadequate tools or equipment, a small business may skimp on quality. Nothing could be more damaging to the long-term success of the business. There are many pressures to underprice in order to win orders, to buy cheap materials and to minimize the time allowed for jobs. However, a reputation for poor quality is easily gained but incredibly hard to overcome. Moreover, many customers will be suspicious of a small business and can be on the look out for quality problems, so you have to be all the more careful not to sell any goods or provide any service which does not come up to adequate quality standards.

However, a small number of new businesses do go to the other extreme, as mentioned in the section on product performance. Quality of a higher standard than the market is prepared to pay for is not going to do you any good in the long run. You will either price yourself out of the market or be forced to sell at a price which does not allow you to make a sufficient profit.

One of the vital roles of market research (as explained in Chapter 2) is to find out exactly how customers in the target market see their needs being satisfied. The level of quality which they find acceptable (and are prepared to pay for) is a crucial element of this research.

3 Style. Styling or conformance with the latest fashion trends, may be the key product variable in many markets. It is becoming an increasingly important influence on the customer's purchase decision across a wide range of products, in industrial as well as consumer markets. A pleasing external appearance to a product can often be created at the design stage at little or no extra cost, and should always be done wherever possible. Even for the most functional of products it may just be the deciding factor.

4 Packaging. It is not just in consumer goods markets that packaging is extremely important. In industrial markets professional and attractive packaging can make all the difference between what may be seen as a desirable product or one that is seen as cheap and shoddy. Packaging has two main purposes. Firstly, it protects the product and ensures that it reaches the customer in exactly the right condition. This is the first priority of packaging and it is especially important if your product is to be delivered to customers via third party carriers. Secondly, the packaging should be made as attractive as possible. It goes without saying that if the product is to be sold from a shop, especially a self-service store, the packaging has to do a lot of the selling for that product. Even in industrial markets the packaging can be seen by many people in the customer's company and can make a considerable impression on them. The packaging says something about your product and your company, and will certainly affect your reputation.

5 Service. All aspects of service play a very important role in that package of benefits which you are offering to the customer. Indeed, if you are in a service industry, the human aspects of service form the basis of your 'product'. For all businesses though, service is a vital element in producing customer satisfaction, or dissatisfaction. You have only to think of the way that you react as a consumer if sales people are rude, unhelpful or inefficient when you are buying something. All businesses need to pay special attention to ensuring that their staff always offer the right kind of service to customers.

A slightly different aspect of service is the extent of the free warranty service that you will offer customers as part and parcel of their purchase. It is obviously necessary to offer at least the level of after-sales service which is the industry norm. For some businesses it may be possible to steal a competitive advantage by offering a better after-sales service than competitors. As a general rule, the more vital the product is to your customers the more highly they will value after-sales service. However, rather than jumping to conclusions on this subject, it would be sensible to do some research and ask a few potential customers exactly what level of after-sales service they would like on offer. As a result of this it is then essential to make full allowance for this level of service in your costings, since the cost of 'free' after-sales service must always be built into the original price of the product. And, in any research you do, find out if customers are prepared to pay the cost of the level of service they say they require.

Pricing decisions

There are two very important aspects to the question of pricing your product or service: how much does it cost me to produce, and how much am I going to sell it for?

The link between these two aspects is by no means as close as many businesses seem to think. In fact, they are related to each other in one respect only. The answer to the first question gives you the base line for deciding the answer to the second question. You obviously cannot, as a general rule, afford to sell your product or service for less than it costs you to supply it. However, how much more than that you should charge is a completely separate question which is answered by looking outwards to the market rather than inwards at your own business. The difference between costing and pricing can be summed up as:

Costing is a matter of fact
Pricing is a matter of policy

A detailed explanation of your business costings will be found in the next chapter (Chapter 11, financial planning). In this chapter we will consider the outward looking aspects of arriving at a market price.

Pricing is a matter of policy. You can charge what you want – in theory. In practice you can only charge what the market will stand, and the real secret of successful pricing is to determine this optimum price which the market will bear which will maximize your profits. Your costings are the starting point. Your objective when determining your prices is to judge how much customers would be prepared to pay for the specific product or service that you are hoping to sell. Arriving at this figure is an art, relying on judgement rather than an exact science for which step-by-step guidelines can be written down. However, a number of relevant factors which should be included in your decision making process are now outlined.

1 **Market research.** As with all the elements of your marketing mix, a major part of your decision should be based on objective market research findings. When you undertake the kind of market research exercises described in Chapter 2, part of your questioning should involve some probing about the price range that customers would be prepared to pay for your particular product or service. You will be surprised how much potential customers will be prepared to be open on this issue, and you certainly do not need to be at all reticent about asking them about prices. However, it is obvious that they are not likely to overstate the price which they would be prepared to pay but rather to understate it, particularly if you are questioning other businesses. Therefore, any price range which emerges as a result of your market research should be regarded as a minimum. Most respondents would almost certainly be prepared to pay slightly more than they indicated in the survey.

2 **The competition.** The first and most important point to make here is that you should not make the prices charged by the competition your yardstick for setting your own prices. There are a number of very good reasons for this. Firstly, it is very unlikely that your marketing mix and the marketing mixes of your competitors are the same in every respect in the eyes of customers, therefore these customers will be prepared to pay more to some companies than to others. Secondly, you do not definitely know that your competitors are charging the optimum price. They may just be copying each other, or they may be mechanically adding a fixed percentage onto their costs. Any business does need to be cautious about charging prices that differ widely from those of the competition, whether they are lower or higher, but in the last resort if your costings show that the price you have worked out would yield an acceptable profit and if your market research indicates that customers would be happy to pay this price then you would be well advised to follow your own results rather than copying your competitors. You might end up pricing according to the 'going rate', but you will have arrived at that decision as a result of independent analysis and not through following your competitors.

3 **Image.** You must always bear in mind that price says something about your product and your business. Price is an indicator of quality. 'The Cheapest and the Best' is one of the most thoughtless

slogans used by any business. It is most unlikely to be true and the vast majority of customers simply don't believe it. If you are marketing a quality product you must ensure that all aspects of your presentation and promotion stress all the benefits of your high quality product or service, thus demonstrating that the relatively high price does actually represent very good value for money. On the other hand if you are deliberately aiming your product at the price sensitive segment of the market then a low price is one of the benefits your promotion should stress strongly. In this case you must double-check your costings to make absolutely certain that you can operate profitably at such low prices.

4 Value for money. Many small new businesses fall into the trap of thinking that they must be cheaper than their competitors to get any business. This reasoning is rarely correct. Customers usually seek good value for money rather than the cheapest price and when they are making a decision to buy a product or service, price is only one of the factors that influences them. Other factors include the quality, reliability and image of the product (and the business supplying it), the availability of the product or service and the effectiveness of the company's promotion. All of these factors together will almost certainly outweigh the price factor.

Place decisions

In the marketing context, 'place' is all about making your product or service *available and accessible* to customers. In short, you want to make it easy for them to buy your product and you must seriously ask yourself whether it really will be easier for customers to buy from you rather than from your competition.

To give one example, a new business may be planning to sell furniture direct from the workshop via mail order marketing. The owner of that business must seriously ask why customers should buy from his inaccessible workshop rather than from the more convenient high street. If lower prices are the only answer, they may not be a sufficient inducement to persuade enough buyers to trek out to an unknown business in an off-beat area. If, however, the business can offer additional benefits such as the option of custom designed furniture, the interest of hand crafted furniture and perhaps the chance to see the craftsman at work on Saturdays, a real alternative to the high street may tempt many customers.

Unless you can offer something unique, it is advisable to concentrate your efforts on making it easier to buy from your business than from the competition. As suggested in Chapter 6, trail blazing, as far as location is concerned, can be a risky policy for a new business.

Promotion decisions

Having developed your product or service according to customers' needs, having worked out a suitable price and having decided exactly how it will be made available and accessible to buyers, there is one more vital marketing challenge facing your business. You need to tell potential customers that your new product exists.

This part of the marketing mix is known as promotion. It is sometimes called 'marketing communications' which is a very apt phrase because it is all about communicating with customers and potential customers. First of all, step back and take an overview of marketing communications to see what your business should be trying to achieve.

A common model which is used to describe the marketing communications process is the 'AIDA' model: Awareness, Interest, Desire, Action.

The aim is to move potential customers from total unawareness of the company and its products through the stages of awareness of the company's existence, interest in the company and its products, recognition of a desire for the product, and finally action, which usually means purchase. The potential customer has become a customer. This is a particularly appropriate model for the new unknown business.

However, most new businesses concentrate too much on the second half of the AIDA model and not enough on the first half. They try to move potential customers straight into buying the product through short-term offers such as low prices. But many customers will not buy from a company they have never heard of, especially important purchases and especially in industrial markets. Most consumers and businesses are rather suspicious of outfits they have never heard of, and as a result the marketing communications of a new company should concentrate initially on spreading awareness, and knowledge about the company and its activities. The initial task therefore is to inform rather than to sell. There are a number of promotional techniques which the new business should consider using to achieve this objective.

1 **Leaflets.** Leaflets are usually a very cost effective way for many new businesses to inform potential customers. Colour glossy leaflets to a set format can be obtained in quantities of 5000 for less than £200. Leaflets should be uncluttered, with one clear message which stands out. In the case of a new business, the message should be simply: 'Look at this new service or product which is now available to help you to . . . . '. Good design and good photography can greatly enhance the impact of your literature but leaflets need not make explicit attempts to sell. In the long run your business will

achieve more sales if you remain content with generating awareness and developing interest at this stage.

Door-to-door distribution of the leaflets may be cost effective. New housing estates, for example, can be very fruitful area for certain services such as gardening and decorating services, or for products like burglar alarms and carpets. You obviously have to consider if the area of leaflet distribution is suitable for your product or service. If it is, this method of promotion can be very effective.

Following the leaflet distribution, an attempt to sell can be made two or three weeks later. Either telephone, or preferably call round in person and simply ask if they are interested. As well as orders you should get some useful market research feedback. If you have distributed many leaflets you should be able to identify the kind of areas which are more responsive. You can then concentrate your personal selling efforts on those areas. You have now developed a formula. Firstly, inform a large number of potential customers. Secondly, follow up a sample personally, and hopefully identify the most fruitful areas in which to concentrate your personal selling efforts.

2 Direct mail. For some businesses it will not be possible to distribute leaflets door to door either due to lack of time or because potential customers are spread over too wide an area. If this is the case you could achieve the same effect of using leaflets to inform potential customers if you send them through the post. Follow-up, probably by telephone initially, can then be carried out following the formula above.

3 Press releases. It may be possible to get local newspapers or specialist magazines to publish something about your business, particularly when it is just starting to trade. About one month before you are due to start trading you should contact local and regional newspapers, all specialist magazines and even local radio. Obviously, the more interesting and newsworthy you can make your press release the more likely it is to be taken up by the media. They like stories that their readers or listeners will be interested in. Therefore you need to think of a story or human interest angle rather than simply presenting the bare facts. After all, another story of yet another new business opening is not a very newsworthy event.

As an example, rather than having as your headline:

'New Fishing Tackle Shop To Open'

you could instead try something like this:

'Miner Achieves 20 Year Ambition To Turn Hobby Into A Business'

One final point about press releases. Many publications will try to persuade you to place an advert in their newspaper or magazine in return for printing your press release. You should resist this. If they think your story is interesting enough they will probably print it anyway.

4 Sales promotions. Defined as 'additional incentives to buy' sales promotions are commonly gimmicks such as 'buy one get one free', or '20% off while this offer lasts'. On the whole, sales promotions, which are usually employed by established businesses to boost sales in the short term, are not particularly appropriate to the needs of a new business. Your objectives at this stage are to generate awareness and build a favourable image for your business. Employing price-cutting tactics from the outset is probably not the right way to build a good image in most markets.

In order to make a big splash when you open you do not have to advertise massive price cuts. There are many other ways of getting noticed. You can have an opening 'event' where wine and possibly a buffet are laid on. You can have an opening competition, which has plenty of scope for generating press coverage, or you may be able to think of an even more original opening event.

5 Advertising. The extent to which you advertise your new business should depend not simply on how much money you have available but also on the suitability of the advertising technique for achieving your marketing communications objectives. It may be that distributing leaflets or staging some special events might be a better way to create an impact with your target customers. However, in some markets, there is no doubt that advertising in the media is effective. There may be a very good trade or special interest magazine, or, if you are concentrating on a well defined geographical area, there might be a very good local newspaper. If you are convinced that advertising is suitable, there are four points you should consider:

a Media. You must make sure that your adverts are placed in appropriate media. In other words, will those media actually reach the kind of people or businesses that you see as your target customers? Don't take this for granted. You can check by asking publications to provide details of their readership. This will tell you the circulation and what kind of people read the newspaper or magazine. You should also check whether the circulation makes advertising cost effective. For example, how many potential customers could you reach with a mail shot for the price of a one page advertisement in a magazine?

b Clear message. Most new businesses have to think up their own adverts and with a limited advertising budget it is vital to make the very best possible use of the space that can be afforded. The most common mistake that small business owners tend to make when designing their own adverts is to try to cram too much information into available space. Too much information can be counter-productive because none is noticed in sufficient depth to be absorbed and remembered. The secret of successful print advertising is to have simple clear messages which stand out.

c Original adverts. An innovative advertising gimmick is a very difficult task to achieve even for large multi-national advertising agencies, but one can obviously think of many well known examples such as the Andrex puppies, the Benson and Hedges 'theme' adverts and the 'Tell Sid' campaign for the British Gas share issue. If you do think of a good original gimmick, the main thing is to stick with it. This kind of advertising does not have instant success but relies on a cumulative build up of the recognition over several years. If you can't think up anything original for your advertising, don't despair, you're not abnormal! Most people don't have good creative ideas. If you just have a straightforward, clear, and simple message it will be perfectly acceptable.

d Classified advertisements. Don't turn your nose up at the classified ads. In local newspapers, specialist magazines and publications like *Exchange and Mart,* classified ads can be very effective. A lot of people buy local newspapers just for the classified ads and religiously wade through the 'miscellaneous sales' columns. A classified ad in the relevant column may be more likely to be noticed by potential customers than a much more expensive display advert in the middle of the newspaper or magazine.

6 Personal selling. The obvious way of getting your message across to potential customers is selling on a one-to-one basis. The ability to be your own best salesman will be an important attribute for all new business owners. Unless you intend to have a partner or co-director who will be responsible for the selling it is a technique which you simply must master. Selling is a technique. Salesmen are made not born. However much you might dislike the idea of selling, if you have enough motivation, which you should have if your livelihood depends on achieving sufficient sales, you can become an adequate salesman.

Unless you are already an experienced salesman, attending a sales training course would appear to be a very wise investment for the vast majority of new business owners. Consult your local college, the Small Firms Service or the Training Agency about the availability of selling courses in your area.

There are many other ways in which you can promote your product or service, from a card in the local shop window to specially made videos or adverts on the backs of buses. There is not the space in this book to explore all the possibilities, but the reader is referred to the companion volume *Successful Marketing for Small Businesses* for additional information.

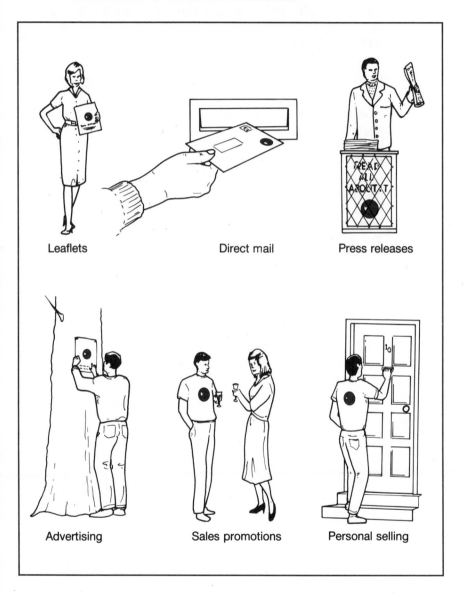

Fig. 10.2 Promoting your small business

Summary

1 Marketing is not about techniques such as selling and advertising but should be seen as a philosophy which pervades the business.

2 This philosophy involves putting customers' needs first and organizing the resources of the business to meet those needs more closely than your competitors meet them.

3 A detailed knowledge of your customers and a complete understanding of their needs is therefore crucial to successful marketing.

4 Small businesses usually need to go further than simply knowing their customers. They have to target precise groups of customers with a specialist product or service that is accurately designed to meet their particular needs.

5 However precisely targeted customers usually have a number of priorities when purchasing a given product or service so a mix of marketing activities is necessary to provide the package of benefits they are looking for. This marketing mix involves managing your product, price, place and promotion in a manner best designed to appeal to your target market.

11 Financial planning

Aims of this chapter

The basic aim of this chapter is to help you to understand the aspects of financial planning which will enable you to distinguish between potentially viable and unviable new businesses. To do this three areas of financial planning need to be examined:

- Start-up costs
- The budget
- The cash flow forecast

Start-up costs

How much does it cost to start your own business: £50, £500 or £10,000? It could be any of these amounts but, as pointed out in Chapter 2, you need to know exactly how much your proposed business will cost to start because you need to be certain that your resources will be adequate. Let's have a look at this by considering the start-up costs of two contrasting businesses.

'Glamorous Nights'

June and Alison are both married. Now that their children have all started school they both feel the need to do something more with their lives and have become keen on the idea of starting their own business. They were both machinists before they left work to have children and they both own industrial sewing machines as a result of their previous employment as outworkers. They need the flexibility to look after the children in the school holidays or if they are ill, and so a small business which they could run from home would be very convenient. Both women have the backing of their husbands and are prepared to invest around £300 each to get the business started.

Having looked at potential products and markets which would be compatible with their previous experience they decided that high quality nightwear for ladies appeared to offer good opportunities. Since they do not want to borrow any money, take any risks, or enter into any long-term commitments at this stage, they plan to buy just enough materials to make a reasonable stock of the small number of designs they have developed and then intend to test their products locally on a 'party plan' basis.

June and Alison have itemized their start-up requirements as follows:

	£
Raw materials	
Fabric	350.00
Thread	22.50
Trimmings	24.00
Polythene bags	9.50
Stationery	
Letter heading and compliments slips	9.95
Envelopes	2.50
Stamps	5.00
Weekly book-keeping book	5.00
Duplicate receipt book	2.00
Duplicate order book	2.00
File for invoices	3.50
Pens and other stationery	5.00
Expenses	
Travel expenses, phone calls, etc	50.00
Promotional costs	
Printing of colour leaflets, inexpensive packaging	145.00
Stamps and envelopes for small local mailshot	20.00
Total start-up costs	**£655.95**

June and Alison do have to be very careful because they want to start their business on a very low budget, but they have been careful not to economize on items that would give an impression of cheapness or low quality. There will be a small range of garments initially but they will be attractively designed, well made out of quality materials and neatly packaged. The leaflets are in colour, have been professionally produced and have attractive photographs. They will be important to induce people to hold the parties, without which sales will not be made. The administration and book-keeping will be methodical and professional. In general they have approached the venture very carefully, creating the most businesslike image possible on the resources they have at their disposal. They can just afford to start the business in this way without borrowing money and will hope to build it up by not paying themselves a wage initially and ploughing back the profits. They have deliberately not formulated long-term aims at this stage, preferring to 'see how it goes'. Even if it is a disaster their potential losses are limited to £655.95.

'Chicago Hamburger House'

On the other hand, the Chicago Hamburger House is going to represent total commitment from husband and wife team Ian and Pam. Ian is going to keep his well-paid job for the time being as the one remaining reminder of their previously secure lifestyle. Otherwise they are determined to do whatever is necessary to achieve their ambition of opening a wine bar and making a success of it. They are prepared to commit all the money they have been able to save and will hope to borrow the rest, offering their house as security.

Ian and Pam have found suitable premises in the town centre which were used for catering purposes by the previous occupant. This was essential, because apart from having to obtain planning permission they do not feel that they could afford to convert premises from scratch. These premises will have many of the kitchen, cooking and toilet facilities which they require. They also have the approval of health, fire and insurance organizations.

However, Ian and Pam want to completely transform the image of the premises both inside and out because they feel that so much of their venture's success will depend on the development of an 'authentic' Chicago theme. They want to make Chicago Hamburger House a fashionable place to go and to be seen in. This will involve getting the decor just right. Ian hs strong views on this subject based on many business trips to the USA but Pam has insisted that they also commission an interior designer who specializes in catering work. Pam will bring the required product knowledge to the venture from her previous employment in the trade, and has decided that some alteration will need to be made to the premises, especially in the kitchen area in order to achieve the level of operating efficiency that their kind of business will require. Initial promotional costs will also be quite high because the 'image' of the restaurant as well as the simple fact of its opening has to be successfully communicated to potential customers.

Ian and Pam have worked out their start-up costs as follows:

Premises, fixtures and fittings	£
Purchase of lease, fixtures and fittings	13,500
Building work to modify premises internally	5,350
New furniture, fixtures and fittings	7,700
Decorating	1,675
Stock	
Initial provisions, food	400
Initial provisions, drink	750
Office expenses	
Furniture and equipment, including computer	8,100
Stationery, including menus	380

continued overleaf

		£
Professional advice		
	Solicitor	900
	Interior designer	1,500
Overheads		
	Advance rent	3,000
	Credit card joining fees	250
Promotional expenses		
	Advertising	7,500
	Opening evening promotional event	1,750
Total start-up costs		£52,755

This is actually a very brief summary of the start-up costs for a venture like the Chicago Hamburger House. Many of the items would have involved fairly lengthy sub-lists of individual costings to arrive at the figures shown.

Working out your initial capital requirements can therefore be a laborious task. Depending on the nature of your proposed business you may need to list different things than the items covered in these two examples. The best way to proceed is to draw up a long list of the items you are likely to need on your first day of trading and then make enquiries about prices with potential suppliers. Some of the sources of advice listed in Chapter 5, for example the Small Firms Service or RDC, should be able to help you with your costings if necessary. Also to reiterate the advice already given in Chapter 2, if you have little personal business experience in the field of your proposed venture, you should get your figures checked by somebody who has.

The budget

Working out your start-up costs shows you the minimum level of investment you need to make in order to get your business off the ground on day one. This may not, however, be an accurate reflection of the level of your financial commitment to that business. If your business is profitable immediately it will not require any more injection of money to keep it afloat, but if it is not profitable immediately it will need more financing than those start-up costs identified in the previous section. June and Alison expect their business to require no additional financing beyond the start-up costs of £655.95. Ian and Pam on the other hand are very unlikely to make money initially. They will have borrowings to repay, staff wages to pay and considerable overheads. It is unlikely that the level of custom will be high enough to cover these costs for the first few months, but as the reputation of the wine bar grows income should begin to overtake expenditure. However, many businesses do envisage an initial loss-making situation because they know it will take time for their selling and promotional activities to result in strong sales, even though they will incur many of their costs from the outset. It is for this reason that budgeting is so important. In addition to your starting up costs you need to estimate how much capital your business will need to see it through to the end of its first or even second year of trading.

The first step then towards projecting the future profitablity of your new business is to draw up a budget. Budgeting is not a difficult concept. It is simply a summary of money coming in and money going out. As individuals we could all draw up a budget showing our own anticipated personal income and expenses over the next week, month or year. Drawing up a business budget may involve more variables, and as a result be more time-consuming to complete, but it is no different in principle. Your profit, quite simply, is the difference between the money your business earns from selling its goods or services and the money your business spends in order to achieve that level of sales. A blank budget form would look something like this:

Budget for year one for Any New Business Ltd

TOTAL SALES		£
DIRECT COSTS		
Purchases (stock or materials)	£	
Labour costs	£	
TOTAL DIRECT COSTS		£
GROSS PROFIT		£
OVERHEADS		
Rent	£	
Rates	£	
Insurance	£	
Loan repayments	£	
Light and heat	£	
Telephone	£	
Postage	£	
Printing and stationery	£	
Bank charges	£	
Professional fees	£	
Repairs and renewals	£	
Credit card charges	£	

continued overleaf

Vehicle expenses:
Petrol £
Servicing and repairs £
Tax and insurance £
Total vehicle expenses £
Advertising and promotion £
TOTAL OVERHEADS £
NET PROFIT £

The problem with drawing up a budget is not understanding the concept but filling it in. Many people new to running a business find it difficult to decide what figures to put in for many of the items, arguing that for a brand new business with no records, no sales and maybe no definite premises the figures must be little more than guesswork. In fact there are many ways of minimizing the guesswork and arriving at sensible estimates.

To examine these, look now at the imaginary case of Tim, a keen amateur athlete who has decided to open a sports shop specializing in running equipment and clothing. The rest of this chapter will follow through the preparation of a budget and cash flow forecast for his proposed venture. He is calling his small business 'Runners' World'.

Runners' World
Budget, year one

1 Sales. Estimating the first year turnover of a new business with no past records to base the figures on is not easy. But, if you are to minimize the risks of investing in your new business venture it has to be done, and it has to be more of an estimation than a guess. First of all it is necessary to build up your own projection of turnover. This does not mean plucking a suitable figure out of the air, such as £100,000 per annum, and then working backwards to decide what you would have to sell to attain this turnover. It has to be tackled the other way round. You must first of all decide what you are likely to achieve in terms of sales. It is reasonable to set yourself demanding targets provided they are realistic, which means having a good idea of how you would achieve them.

There are a number of ways in which you might substantiate your own ideas of projected turnover.

a Detailed projections. First of all you must think through your own ideas of expected sales in some detail. In Tim's case, just how many pairs of expensive running shoes would he have to sell? How many pairs of shorts and track suits, how many cagoules and holdalls? Do sales of that volume seem sensible for the first year of a new business? Having convinced yourself you then need to see if anybody else supports your views.

b Private enquiries. It may be feasible to contact some similar businesses to your own proposed venture, explain what you are planning to do and ask for some friendly advice. Provided that the business you choose is not located in an area where you are likely to open up in direct competition you will probably find people very helpful. Tim had used his running contacts to gain some introductions to two existing owners of specialist athletic shops in other parts of the country. They had proved very helpful, but both had agreed that Tim's projections of £90,000 first year turnover were over optimistic. They felt that a figure of £75,000 would be more realistic. Tim had also spoken to some similar but non-competing specialist shops in his home town. He chose an angling shop and a watersports shop, both specialist sports shops but not future competitors. They were currently turning over in excess of £75,000 and said that since the town was a regional centre Tim could expect to attract trade from a wide radius, provided he promoted his business well.

c Colleges. Universities, polytechnics or colleges in your area may offer courses, as described in Chapter 5, or might offer practical help to local businesses. Tim's local polytechnic offered market research surveys, carried out by marketing students under the supervision of lecturers at a fraction of the normal commercial cost. Tim commissioned a survey and the results were interesting in that they showed more interest than he had expected from non-serious runners, such as 'lunchtime' joggers, who nevertheless were interested in purchasing the 'right' gear.

d Professional advisers. Tim then consulted three professional advisers. First of all he went to his Local Enterprise Agency, then his accountant and finally his bank manager. All were impressed with Tim's work and did not think he could have researched his figures any more thoroughly.

As a result of all these enquiries Tim decided that £75,000 turnover for his first year was a reasonably safe bet. He still felt he could do better, and was determined to prove to the two pessimistic shop owners that he could achieve his initial target of £90,000. However, for financial planning purposes, he would stick with the cautious figure of £75,000.

2 Purchases. Once Tim has projected a sales figure it is a relatively easy task to work out the cost of the stock necessary to achieve those sales. This will depend on the amount of mark-up on the items Tim is selling, which is simply the difference between the price he buys the stock in at and the price at which he sells it. For example, if he buys an item at £10 and sells it at £15, the mark-up is 50 per cent. In which case he has made £5 gross profit on that item. That £5 profit on a selling price of £15 represents a gross margin of 33.33 per cent. In fact, most of the items that Tim will sell carry a higher mark-up than 50 per cent, but he was advised by all the shop owners he consulted to work on a more conservative margin to allow for periodical sales of shop soiled or slow moving items, commissions on credit card sales, and pilferage. Tim therefore decided that a 33.33 per cent margin was realistic. If Tim achieves a turnover of £75,000 on a margin of 33.33 per cent, the cost of the stock he would need to buy in to reach that turnover would be 66.66 per cent of £75,000, i.e. £50,000.

In the first year Tim is not planning to employ anybody. His wife will help in the shop on Saturdays and other members of his family have promised support. He can therefore work out his gross profit as follows:

Runners' World: year one profit

TOTAL SALES		£75,000
DIRECT COSTS		
Purchases	£50,000	
Labour	£ –	
TOTAL DIRECT COSTS		£50,000
GROSS PROFIT		£25,000

This will not, however, be Tim's final profit figure because he will have more costs than the figure for stock which had been entered above. He will also have overheads and must therefore work those out next.

3 Known overheads. As far as overheads are concerned the best place to start is with definite figures. If you have already identified premises some of the overheads associated with running those premises will be known to you. Although Tim had not yet found suitable retail premises he had made extensive enquiries at local estate agents, has been to look round several empty shops and had spoken to a number of local shopkeepers. As a result he has a very good idea of the cost of running a shop of the size he has in mind, reasonably close to the town centre. Tim's known overheads are as follows:

a Rent. In a good location shop rents in Tim's local town seem to be about £8 per square foot. Tim has decided that he needs about 500 square feet of sales area so his annual rent is going to be around £4000.

b Rates. Tim has approached the local council and has been told that 500 square feet of shop space on the high street would cost him a rates bill of about £825 per annum.

c Insurance. From his insurance broker Tim obtained an accurate costing of £225 for his annual insurance premium for a retail insurance package for the kind of business he had in mind.

d Loan repayments. Having worked out his start-up costs Tim has been for a general chat with his bank manager and has been informed that the repayments on the size of loan he had in mind would amount to £180 per month or £2160 per annum.

4 Estimated overheads. The overheads we will look at next are not known, they will have to be estimated. They are sometimes known as variable overheads because they tend to vary with the volume of business that is done. An existing business can estimate these overheads very accurately since it should be easy to find how much they cost the business in the previous year. A new business does not have any past records to base its figures on but there are ways of estimating these amounts.

a Light and heat. Tim has asked other shopkeepers what their bills tend to be and as a result of these enquiries expects electricity charges of approximately £475 per annum.

b Telephone. Tim will have a relatively small number of suppliers and most of his other calls will be local, so he has estimated an annual figure of £300 for his telephone bills.

c Postage. Tim has allowed £150, or nearly £3 per week, for postage.

d Printing and stationery. Leaflets, carrier bags, receipt pads, price stickers, and special offer posters will be among Tim's printing requirements during the year. He has made enquiries concerning costs and has decided to budget for £250 in his first year of trading.

e Bank charges. The bank has advised Tim that provided he does not go overdrawn, £100 should be sufficient to cover his first year's bank charges.

f Professional fees. The accountant is proposing to charge Tim a basic annual fee of £250 for preparing his accounts from a set of well kept books. Tim has also allowed £150 for consulting his solicitor over the terms of any shop lease that he might sign, making a total of £400 for professional fees.

g Repairs and renewals. Tim is determined not to take on run down premises and will save money by doing much of the decoration himself. Repairs and renewals do, however, cover a wide range of possibilities since anything in the shop might need repairing or replacing at some stage. He has decided to budget £250 for his first year.

h Vehicle expenses. Much as he would like to, Tim will not be splashing out on a big new car to celebrate the opening of his new business. He has calculated that the running costs for his existing car will be £550 for petrol, £300 for servicing and £260 for tax and insurance, making a total budget of £1110.

5 Budgeted overheads. It could be argued that advertising and promotion are budgeted overheads rather than estimated overheads, although it is possible to increase or reduce your advertising expenditure as you choose provided you accept that less promotion is likely to lead, in the long run at least, to a drop in sales. However, most companies do have a budget for such items, and they set a limit to their spending. Other types of overheads may also fall into this category, such as training expenditure and trade association fees.

As a new retailer in a competitive market Tim has decided that promotional activities will be very important for getting his business established. He has decided to allow £2000 for advertising which will be in the regional press and in specialist running magazines. He hopes to supplement his advertising with the maximum amount of free publicity he can generate from press releases and the staging of events. He has therefore allocated £1750 to promotional expenditure such as sponsoring local events and organizing 'runners evenings' with films, guest speakers, etc, during the winter. His total budget for advertising and promotion is therefore £3750.

We can therefore list Runners' World's overheads as follows:

Runners' World: year one overheads

Known overheads		
Rent		£4,000
Rates		825
Insurance		225
Loan repayments		2,160
Estimated overheads		
Light and heat		475
Telephone		300
Postage		150
Printing and stationery		250
Bank charges		100
Professional fees		400
Repairs and renewals		250
Vehicle expenses:		
Petrol	£550	
Servicing and repairs	300	
Tax and insurance	260	
Total vehicle expenses		1,110
Budgeted overheads		
Advertising and promotion		3,750
TOTAL OVERHEADS		£13,995

It is this sum that Tim must deduct from his gross profit in order to ascertain his projected net profit for year one.

TOTAL SALES	£75,000
TOTAL DIRECT COSTS	50,000
GROSS PROFIT	25,000
TOTAL OVERHEADS	13,995
NET PROFIT	£11,005

6 Drawings. Although he has put nothing for his labour costs, Tim will certainly need to pay himself something. As a sole trader, Tim will be the owner rather than an employee of his business and therefore his pay will be known as 'drawings'. This refers to the fact that they are advance drawings on his profits. Tim has decided that the least he can manage on personally is £100 per week (and he will have to find his own self-employed National Insurance contribution out of that, which will set him back over £5 per week), and he therefore proposes to pay himself £5200 per annum. If this is deducted from his net profit figure he is left with a sum of £5805, which can be called 'retained profit', money to be ploughed back into the business to help its future growth. In reality, however, it means that Tim's overheads, including his own drawings are £19,195 per annum.

7 Breakeven. Let's assume, for ease of arithmetic, that Tim's total overheads are £20,000 per annum. This figure can then be used to work out the breakeven sales figure for Runners' World. If Tim's average gross margin is 33.33 per cent the breakeven calculation is as follows:

$$\frac{\text{Overheads} \quad £20,000}{\text{Gross margin} \quad 33.33\%} \times 100 = £60,000$$

If he is to cover his overheads and pay himself £100 per week, Tim must achieve sales of at least £60,000 per annum. Above that figure one third of all his turnover will be extra profit for the business. Therefore, if he achieved his personal target of £90,000 turnover, that extra £30,000 above breakeven would yield £10,000 profit for the business over and above Tim's drawings. By dividing the breakeven figure by 12 you arrive at Tim's monthly breakeven target of £5000 – the minimum turnover Tim needs to achieve each month if he is not to lose money.

A carefully prepared budget represents a very good estimation of the performance of your business in its first year of trading. Although some new businesses, started with large capital investments, are not expected to move into profit for two or even three years, most people starting a business will want to be confident that their business will be profitable in its first year. However, even though Runners' World is projected to make a good profit in its first year of trading, it cannot be certain that it will operate cash inflow each month during that year without completing a cash flow forecast.

The cash flow forecast

The amount of money you need to start a business really needs to be divided into two categories: the money you need *before* you start trading, and the money you need *after* you start trading.

The first category referred to in this chapter was start-up costs. This includes all the things a business needs to possess on the first day of trading if it is going to operate on a proper basis.

The second category can be described as 'working capital'. Many new businesses do not make a profit from day one. A new manufacturing business may have to pay wages from day one, pay rent, rates, electricity, run vehicles and buy raw materials. It will have to get its production going, and build up its sales, maybe with the help of a hefty promotional budget. The goods it does sell may go out on credit with payment coming in one or two months later.

In order to work out his working capital requirement Tim will need to complete a cash flow forecast. If the larger part of his sales and gross profits are coming in in the second half of the year, Tim may need extra working capital in the first half of the year. Moreover, even if Runners' World consistently makes profits it may have much of its cash tied up in stock like running shoes and track suits on the shelves and may therefore have a working capital requirement.

Cash flow forecast forms

A blank cash flow forecast form is shown on pages 168-9. It looks complicated but in reality is nothing more than a lot of monthly budgets joined together. As you can see, the months are listed across the top, and down the side are all the figures you will have already produced for the year for your budget. All you have to do is to break them down into monthly receipts and payments. The only additional entries come in the bottom few lines which enable your cash surplus or deficit at the end of each month to be carried forward to the next month.

It is worth noting that all the high street banks produce their own cash flow forecast forms. They are all basically similar to the one shown overleaf but each may have slight differences in format or wording. If you are planning to approach one of the banks for a loan it would be sensible at this stage to prepare your cash flow forecast on the printed form produced by your own bank. These forms should be freely available from the enquiries desk of your local branch.

Runners' World

Filling in the cash flow forecast

1 Sales. It is difficult in the first year of a new business to allocate your projected sales on a monthly basis. You can however predict factors like seasonal peaks and troughs in demand. Tim knows that he will sell more in the summer months when the athletics season is in full swing, and he would expect to do quite well out of Christmas shoppers in December, but he would not expect good figures for his first three months of trading. If you use the cash flow forecast form from one of the banks you will notice that it contains twice as many columns because each month has a 'budget' column and an 'actual' column. The 'actual' column is for you to add the real figures after each month of trading. This allows you to update the picture as you go along.

2 Goods for resale. Tim would expect to be allowed normal 30 day credit terms by his suppliers, therefore his cash outflow for purchases will occur one month after he reorders the goods. This is an important factor in Tim's positive cash flow predictions since he receives cash payment for his sales but does not pay for his purchases until the end of the month after he receives them. An additional problem as far as purchases are concerned is how to handle the opening stock. In Tim's case he has decided to use his personal savings topped up by a bank loan to purchase his opening stock so his cash flow forecast will show only payments for replacement stock and monthly loan repayments.

3 Rent. It is common for rents for retail premises to be payable quarterly in advance.

4 Rates. Rates are payable in two instalments, at the end of June and at the end of October for the year commencing April 1st. If, as in this example, you occupy premises in January there would be a three month rates bill to pay for the remainder of that financial year. Some authorities may allow commercial rates to be paid on a monthly standing order basis. This is worth checking since it does ease the cash flow burden.

A cash flow forecast form

	Jan	Feb	Mar	Apr
Income: Sales				
Expenditure: Goods for resale				
OVERHEADS				
Rent				
Rates				
Insurance				
Loan repayments				
Light and heat				
Telephone				
Postage				
Printing and stationery				
Bank charges				
Professional fees				
Repairs and renewals				
Vehicle expenses:				
Petrol				
Tax, insurance and servicing				
Advertising				
Promotional expenses				
Drawings				
Total expenditure (overheads and stock)				
Net surplus for month or				
Net deficit for month				
Cash Balance B/F from previous month				
Cash Balance B/F to next month				

May	Jun	Jul	Aug	Sept	Oct	Nov	Dec	Total

5 Insurance. Tim will need insurance from day one so the whole budget figure has been entered in January. It may be possible to pay insurance in three or four equal monthly instalments spread over the first four months of the year. This would ease the cash flow problem for Tim, but interest is likely to be charged and almost certainly at a higher rate than that charged by the bank.

6 Loan Repayments. Most business developments loans have a fixed rate of interest over a fixed term, so monthly repayments never alter.

7 Light and heat. Just like domestic fuel bills, the two winter quarters result in significantly higher charges than the summer periods. A little common sense is all that Tim requires here.

8 Telephone and postage. Unless he has good reason to do otherwise, Tim's budgeted figures for these items should be split equally on a quarterly and monthly basis respectively.

9 Printing and stationery. Tim has decided to allocate 40 per cent of his budget to January for a lot of basic printed items, a further 40 per cent to June mainly for items ordered in connection with summer promotions and 20 per cent to the autumn for replacement stationery, bags, sale posters, etc.

10 Bank charges. These charges should also be split equally through the year, although Tim's budget forecast already needed amending since he had to add interest charges to the January, February and March figures when he will expect to be overdrawn at the bank. The total amount in the final column is therefore higher than that shown on his budget.

11 Professional fees. Of the £400 Tim budgeted for professional fees, £150 was allocated to legal fees for advice on any shop lease which Tim would have to sign in order to start his business. The £250 allocated to accountancy fees does not appear on this forecast because it will not be paid until after the accountant has audited Runners' World's first year results.

12 Repairs and renewals. The cost of repairs and renewals can vary enormously from one business to another depending on the nature of the premises and the sort of equipment used by the business. It will also depend upon how much work the owner is prepared to do himself. It is difficult to predict this kind of expenditure so Tim has spread it evenly through the year.

13 Vehicle expenses. As far as petrol is concerned, Tim has allowed for more motoring in the summer months. His insurance and road tax fall in January and February respectively and the estimated budget for servicing and repairs has been evenly split into four.

14 Advertising and promotional expenses. Tim intends to allocate most of his advertising and promotional expenditure to the summer months to coincide with the maximum interest in athletics. For his first year however he does need to devote a sizeable chunk of advertising spending to the opening of the shop and will hold an opening promotion. He also plans to promote the shop strongly in December to attract the Christmas trade.

15 Drawings. Drawings can simply be allocated on a regular monthly basis.

16 Cash balances. The first task is to add up all expenditure for the month. Despite including no payments for stock, Tim's expenditure at £3453 is quite high for January and well exceeds his expected sales of £2000. By deducting total expenditure from sales a figure for net surplus or net deficit for the month is found. Tim will have a negative cash flow of −£1453 in his first month, and will therefore need to approach his bank for an overdraft facility. It will be March before his account moves into credit. Each month you can see that the cash balance is carried forward to the next month. The surplus of deficit for the month is added onto (or subtracted from) the initial cash balance to produce a new cash balance to carry forward to the next month.

Runners' World's completed forecast is shown overleaf.

Runners' World
Assessment of cash flow forecast

Completing your first cash flow forecast is only a starting point. It may tell you that your initial thoughts were too pessimistic or too optimistic. Tim appears to be erring on the side of overcaution. That is a good thing at this stage but if his new business turns out to be capable of generating as much cash as his forecast suggests he should have some views about how he might use that cash. There are a number of possibilities:

1 Borrowings. Tim could decide to borrow less money in the form of a bank loan to start his business and use an overdraft facility instead for part of his borrowing requirement. He could deduct £5000 from his bank loan and add it to his overdraft facility and still clear his overdraft by the middle of the summer. This would be the cheapest way of borrowing money.

2 Reinvestment. Tim could plan to plough back his cash surpluses into the business, especially if he feels that his shop could

Completed cash flow forecast for Runners' World (*all figures in £s*)

	Jan	Feb	Mar	Apr
Income: Sales	2000	3500	4500	6000
Expenditure: Goods for resale		1333	2333	3000
OVERHEADS				
Rent	1000			1000
Rates	200			
Insurance	225			
Loan repayments	180	180	180	180
Light and heat			155	
Telephone			75	
Postage	12	13	12	13
Printing and stationery	100			
Bank charges	28	35	19	8
Professional fees	150			
Repairs and renewals	25	25	20	20
Vehicle expenses:				
Petrol	40	40	40	45
Tax, insurance and servicing	160	100	75	
Advertising	600			200
Promotional expenses	300			
Drawings	433	433	433	433
Total expenditure (overheads and stock)	3453	2159	3342	4899
Net surplus for month or		1341	1158	1101
Net deficit for month	1453			
Cash Balance B/F from previous month		−1453	−112	1046
Cash Balance B/F to next month	−1453	−112	1046	2147

May	Jun	Jul	Aug	Sept	Oct	Nov	Dec	Total
7500	8500	9500	7000	7000	6000	5000	8500	75000
4000	5000	5666	6333	4666	4666	4000	3333	44330
		1000			1000			4000
	412				412			1024
								225
180	180	180	180	180	180	180	180	2160
	90			90			140	475
	75			75			75	300
12	13	12	13	12	13	12	13	150
	100				50			250
8	9	8	8	9	8	8	9	157
								150
20	20	20	20	20	20	20	20	250
50	55	55	50	50	45	40	40	550
	75			75			85	570
200	200	200	200	200			200	2000
250	300	300		300			300	1750
433	433	433	433	433	433	433	433	5196
5153	6962	7874	7237	6110	6827	4693	4828	63537
2347	1538	1626		890		307	3672	
			237		827			
2147	4494	6032	7658	7421	8311	7484	7791	
4494	6032	7658	7421	8311	7484	7791	11463	11463

benefit from a wider range of stock than that which he will initially carry.

3 **Drawings.** He could spend some of the surplus on himself. His drawings are very low. Even allowing for the 'perks' of self-employment such as virtually free motoring, and involvement in his hobby of athletics at the expense of the business, Tim is very badly paid. If he doubled his salary, paying himself around the national average, a very large part of his cash surplus would disappear.

The value of the cash flow forecast

The great value of a cash flow forecast is that it allows you to indulge in these 'what if' scenarios. This is an important planning aid as it enables you to predict the outcome of alternative policies or decisions on stock levels, types of finance, advertising and sales, personal drawings, and so on. If your cash flow forecast is on a spreadsheet on a computer the possibilities for such planning are vastly increased since instant changes in results can be produced from each change made to an entry on the spreadsheet. The first step for any prospective business is simply to complete a manual forecast which is as realistic as you can possibly make it.

Summary

1 Start-up costs cover all the items you need to operate your business properly on the first day of trading. They can vary enormously from one business to another and need to be worked out very carefully in order to ensure that you can afford to start the kind of business you are proposing.

2 Having decided that you can afford to start a particular business, you also need to assure yourself that it is likely to be a profitable venture. To do this you need to work out a realistic budget for your first year of trading. New businesses which will take more than one year to become profitable will need to budget for that extended period.

3 To complete the financial planning picture a cash flow forecast must be drawn up. This will identify any working capital requirements that the business is likely to have and provides a very useful framework for analysing alternative policies.

12 Raising capital

Aims of this chapter

As a result of completing Chapter 11 you will now know if you need additional finance to start your business, and if so, how much. This chapter will examine:

- Alternative ways of raising that money
- The bank's attitude to lending money to small businesses
- The importance of presenting your case in the right way

Alternative forms of finance

Bank loans

This is by far the most common way of raising money for a new business. The banks have a wide variety of loans available and are constantly introducing new ideas, so it is advisable to check on the types of loan currently on offer from all the main high street banks. There are four main types of loan:

1 Overdraft. A straightforward bank overdraft is usually the cheapest way of borrowing money. It is not because the rate of interest is lower but because you are paying interest only on the amount by which you are overdrawn at any one time. Every time you pay money into the bank when you receive payment from a customer your overdraft will go down. By collecting money in efficiently and by avoiding paying money out until you have to it is often possible to reduce your overdraft significantly on a day-to-day basis. Overdrafts therefore represent the most cost effective way of borrowing money, so you should try to get as much of your finance as possible in this way. Unfortunately the banks like you to use overdraft facilities only for short-term borrowing. They are unlikely to give you much, if any of your start-up capital on overdraft. They will however allow an overdraft to cover short-term working capital requirements of the kind highlighted in the previous chapter.

2 Business development loan. This is the usual business loan that most people will use if they borrow money from the bank for their start-up capital. The repayments will be made monthly, commonly spread over three to five years, and the repayments will commence the first month after the money is borrowed. Interest rates will usually be fixed over the whole period of the loan which is good for financial planning since it avoids the monthly repayments fluctuating with changes in the bank's base rate. This type of loan will normally require security or a personal guarantee and the bank will probably expect you to risk some of your money too, preferably on a one-to-one basis, for example, £1 of your money for every £1 you wish to borrow from the bank. However, all these criteria generally have room for negotiation. This type of loan is usually the easiest to secure and, of the four types outlined here, the least expensive.

3 Asset loans. It may be possible to borrow up to 100 per cent of the capital required for business assets such as premises, vehicles, machinery, fixtures and fittings.

4 The Loan Guarantee Scheme. Under this scheme the government guarantees a large proportion of the loan (currently 70 per cent). This means that the borrower has only to personally guarantee or provide security for the remaining 30 per cent of the loan. The price for limiting your liability in this way is a slightly higher rate of interest, which is, in effect, an insurance premium for the 70 per cent which the government guarantees. The scheme is designed to help small businesses with little or no track record and perhaps relatively little security to offer but the absence of security does not prevent a loan from being considered. You can apply for a loan under this scheme through any of the major high street banks.

Leasing

This is one way of getting part of your borrowing requirement covered and therefore of reducing the amount of bank lending you need to ask for.

Any capital equipment could be funded by a leasing deal, including items such as cash registers, production machinery or catering equipment. One additional advantage of such an arrangement could be the inclusion of design or other consultancy services in the deal. For example, the supplier of leased shop fittings may also give professional advice on the interior design of the shop.

Company vehicles are very often acquired under leasing arrangements. The total cost of buying and running your own vehicle needs to be compared with the cost of leasing. The rate of interest charged by leasing agreements will often be higher than under a basic bank loan, making leasing seem less attractive. If, however, your capital requirement is large, the bank may prefer you to spread your borrowings over more than one source of finance. As already stated in Chapter 3, one can question the logic of this policy. There seems little point from the borrower's point of view to use a more expensive form of finance unless you really have no alternative.

If you do opt for leasing to cover any part of your borrowings it is essential to shop around for the best deal. Compare the rates of interest and the terms of the agreement. It is also fair to say that for some companies, leasing may offer tax advantages. Thus, as you can see, leasing can become very complex, and you should always seek advice from an impartial professional source such as your accountant.

Venture capital

This option entails finding a backer who invests in your business. Rather than lending you the money the backer buys a stake in your business, which means that it is an option only for limited companies. The advantage of venture capital is that since it is not a loan you have no monthly repayments to make, no interest charges to bear and no requirement to offer security or personal guarantees. Under many venture capital schemes you also gain the benefit of an injection of management expertise into your company since many investors will demand a seat on the board. The other side of this coin is that you relinquish some control over your own company and reduce your own stake in it. This is a value judgement that each individual must make, but, in general, the more ambitious the scheme the more seriously venture capital must be taken. However, venture capital should be seen as a means of raising substantial, rather than small amounts of funding – usually six or seven figure sums. Further details of venture capital and organizations which provide it can be obtained from:

The British Venture Capital Association, 1 Surrey St,
London WC2N 2PS. Tel: 01 286 5702.

There are two specific examples of venture capital that should be highlighted:

1 The Business Expansion Scheme. This is a government scheme which gives a tax incentive to individuals to invest money in private companies. Tax relief is available at the highest rate paid by the investor provided he leaves his money in the company for at least five years. This scheme precludes investors from taking an active part in the company and imposes certain other restrictions, but it may make it financially attractive for someone to invest in your company. You may have a relative, a contact or you can even advertise for a backer under this scheme.

2 3i (Investors in Industry). 3i is a major player in the venture fund market, giving equal consideration to the requirements of the smaller company. Compared with many sources of finance it takes a long-term view of its investments and does not interfere much in the affairs of financed companies. 3i has a number of regional offices but further details can be obtained from:

Investors in Industry plc, 91 Waterloo Rd, London SE1 8XP. Tel: 01 928 7822.

Creditors

The cheapest of all ways of borrowing money is borrowing from your suppliers – your trade creditors. You can often have quite large sums outstanding and, unless you contravene their terms of business, need not pay a penny in interest charges. In retailing you would receive payment on the day you make each sale whereas you will buy stock on credit. In manufacturing that will not be the case, and often your debtors will exceed your creditors. However, by sound financial management (as suggested in the section on leasing) you can effectively reduce your working capital requirements.

On a warning note, however, don't try to use trade creditors as banks. Apart from jeopardizing future supplies you could put

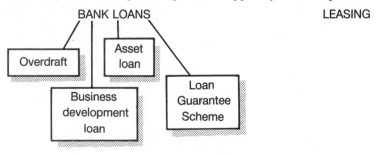

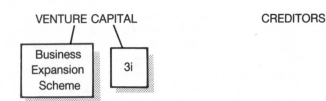

Fig. 12.1 Raising finance

yourself in a potentially dangerous position if you allow large debts to suppliers to accumulate. It is also relevant to point out that new businesses will find it difficult to get expensive credit from suppliers until they build up a track record or can offer good credit references.

The bank's attitude

Whatever your source of finance you need to understand the position of the lender. Since most small businesses use a high street bank for borrowing, at least as a first port of call, it is worth looking at things from their point of view. There are a number of aspects to consider:

1 Customers matter. You are a very important person to the bank. You are a customer and, as pointed out in Chapter 10, all businesses depend upon satisfied customers. Don't approach the bank with any feelings of trepidation.

2 Banks lend money! Banks make money by lending money and charging interest. They are therefore constantly looking for opportunities to lend money, just as your business will constantly look for opportunities to make sales. To the bank lending money is making a sale, though, of course, bank managers have also been trained to err on the side of caution.

3 The bank wants you to succeed. If your business prospers and grows it will have more money passing through its bank account, and will pay more bank charges. It may become a valuable customer for some of the bank's peripheral services such as insurance or export services and it may want additional, larger loans in the future. For all these reasons you should approach the bank with confidence.

4 Bad risks. This of course is not the whole story. No business wants customers at *any* cost. Good customers will be your life blood; bad ones can be potentially lethal to any business. One of the qualities that banks most value in their managers is their ability to identify the kind of customer who may develop into a bad debt. You therefore need to create the impression that you will be a good customer. It might also be the case that the banks in your town have different attitudes towards lending, so it could pay you to shop around.

5 How much are you risking? If you are expecting the bank manager to take a risk and lend money to you it seems reasonable for him to expect you to be prepared to take a risk as well. There are three levels of commitment that the bank might expect of you:

a Your contribution. The banks see their role as funding the part of the enterprise that you cannot meet from your own resources. They do not want to be the major owners of your business. They will therefore expect to see that you are willing to invest in the business, but other ways of emphasizing your contribution such as your willingness to leave a secure job or take an intital cut in salary, will help to demonstrate your commitment.

b Personal guarantee. The bank manager may ask you to demonstrate your confidence in your proposed business by giving a personal guarantee to repay the money. For a small to medium sized loan, at worst, you could be left with paying it off for some years to come if your business failed – very unfortunate but not catastrophic. If you give a personal guarantee for a larger loan the consequences of business failure could be personal bankruptcy. If you are not prepared to take this risk you would have to consider other forms of finance such as venture capital or possibly the Loan Guarantee Scheme.

c Security. For larger loans the bank may want you to pledge security to cover all or the greater part of that loan. This security could be anything that the banks could take possession of and sell in order to recover their money. The most obvious asset is your house. For people with family responsibilities this is a commitment to be avoided as it could place a great strain on everyone whenever things seem to be going badly for the business. Other items of security such as stocks and shares, life policies or third party guarantees could be explored with your bank.

6 Making the right impression. Of course, if the bank manager is not confident in the success of your proposed business venture he won't give you a loan simply because you offer security and are therefore a good risk. More important than security from his point of view is the confidence you inspire. This is all about presenting your case correctly and the remainder of this book will be devoted to the subject.

Presenting your case

There are two aspects to presenting your case:

Personal presentation

The bank manager needs to have confidence in you as a person. He needs to be convinced that you have the personal ability to carry out the business plans that you are proposing. This means that for any visit to a bank where you are seeking finance you must have done your homework so that you can talk confidently and competently about your plans. You must also be very enthusiastic.

After all, if you are not confident in the success of your business, why should anybody else be?

Written presentation

Confidence is admirable. Being a good talker is also useful. Neither will secure you a loan. In the final analysis the bank manager will make his decision objectively on the basis of written proposals that you make. This is your business plan, but as well as being a good plan, sound in its financial and marketing assumptions, it must be presented in the right way. Presentation can make a very big difference. A comprehensive and well presented plan, in the kind of format relished by the banks, can make a very strong impression. After all, for a new business venture with no track record, the bank manager has nothing else to go on. The final chapter of this book will cover the writing of your business plan.

Summary

1 There are many ways of raising business finance but for most typical new businesses a conventional bank loan will remain the favourite method.

2 The larger your proposed loan, and the more it would put your personal assets at risk if personally guaranteed, the more you may be interested in venture capital.

3 Banks must be approached in a confident manner, partly to create a good impression but also because you are a potentially important customer to them.

4 You do need to be able to convince the bank manager that you are a good risk and that your proposed business venture has good prospects.

5 The preparation of an excellent business plan is the best way of convincing the bank manager.

13 The business plan

Aims of this chapter

The basic aim of this chapter is to help you to bring together all the important aspects of starting your business and to put them down on paper in a coherent plan. We will look at:

- The importance of planning
- Writing the plan
- The presentation of the plan

The importance of planning

All successful businessmen and professional advisers will stress the importance of good planning. For example, a family going abroad for a fortnight will spend a lot of time choosing the right holiday with suitable accommodation, recreational facilities and climate. They will plan the journey and perhaps a list of things to do or sights to see on holiday. They will take out insurance against illness, theft and possibly motoring insurance. They will do some financial planning to ensure that they can afford both the capital cost of the holiday and the day-to-day costs whilst abroad, and they will organize travellers cheques or foreign currency to cover these 'working capital' requirements. Many people save for their holiday, others take out a loan to pay for it. On their return everybody analyses their holiday. Was it enjoyable, was it good value for money, would they go there again? This analysis is actually the first stage of planning next year's holiday – the cycle has begun again.

It is not an exaggeration to say that some people start a business with less planning than the average family devotes to its two weeks on the Mediterranean. When you think about what is at stake in starting and running a business and about the diverse range of activities which need to be managed efficiently, the need to give attention to planning should be obvious. Planning is a vital element for the success of your business. It is not something you do only if you need a bank loan, although the kind of plan outlined in this chapter would be ideal to support a loan application. Anybody starting a business must write a business plan. It will give you something concrete to discuss with your accountant or other professional advisers. It will give you financial targets to aim for, tasks to achieve and it can be a yardstick for monitoring the progress of your business.

Writing the business plan

Background of the business

You should start your business plan by giving some background details. As a new venture your business won't have much of a history but there will be background information that could be of great interest to a bank manager or adviser. You should cover the following:

1 Reasons for wanting to start a business. This covers your motives and your personal suitability for running a business (discussed in Chapter 1).

2 Your business idea. Having decided to start a business explain briefly what attracted you initially to this particular business idea. Just give brief details here and then expound on your market research findings in the 'marketing' category (see later).

3 Preparations to date. State how long you have been planning your business venture and whether you have already taken any specific steps towards starting it.

The people in the business

This section of the plan is of vital importance. One of the main factors in the decision about whether or not to lend money is often the bank manager's judgement about whether the people running the business have the makings of successful businessmen. If several partners or directors are involved the details below will need to be completed for each one.

1 Name.

2 Age.

3 Marital and family status.

4 Qualifications and courses attended.

5 Health record.

6 Employment history since leaving full-time education.

7 Position in your business. Even as a sole trader you should write something here because as time goes on you may plan to specialize in certain aspects of running the business. If you have partners the roles of each should be made clear.

8 Experience and knowledge of your industry. You will hopefully have covered part of this in point 6 but you can elaborate on your employment history by demonstrating exactly why your experience is relevant to your new business. You may be able to include other advantages you may have such as relatives in the trade, or a long running recreational interest in the activity.

9 Employees. Give details of any employees you plan to take on from the start of trading. Explain your ideas about how your staff will need to be strengthened in the future.

Don't be afraid of highlighting areas of weakness. It will be seen as a good thing if you have the ability to recognize them. If you are vulnerable in any key areas you should be able to show a contingency plan to be implemented in the case of illness for example, or you might highlight a training need to overcome a skill gap.

The product or service

Your bank manager will obviously want to know as much as possible about the product or service you intend to sell. Give him a comprehensive description, without getting too technical, so that he can build up a good understanding of the product or service upon which your success will depend. In particular you should mention:

1 Individual products. If you are to sell a range of products or services you should itemize each one and state what proportion of your turnover you expect each to contribute. Try to be as accurate as possible.

2 Distinctiveness. In what way is your product different from those products sold by the competition? You should highlight any aspects of your product, and the way you will sell it or the service you will provide, which could distinguish you from the competition.

3 Future developments. Give details of any new products or services you hope to introduce in the future.

Marketing

However good your product it is essential to convince the bank manager: that there is a market for it; and that you will be able to do a good job of selling and promoting to that market. Chapter 2 covered the first point and Chapter 10 the second. Your plan should include details of:

1 The geographical location of your market.

2 The size of your market. For many new businesses this is virtually impossible to quantify, and if it is obviously large, for example, the market for childrens' clothing, there is no problem in this respect. But for some new business ideas, for example making kits to convert Volkswagon Beetles into beach buggies, there may be some doubt over the adequacy of the market's size.

3 Market share. If the market is small your ability to gain a significant share of it will be critical. You need to be able to support any expectations of gaining a large share quickly.

4 Market growth. Will growing demand aid your own growth plans, and if so can you provide any evidence of the buoyancy of your market?

5 Customers. Describe a typical customer, whether another business or a consumer, and outline any evidence you have that such customers will be interested in your product or service.

6 Competitors. Describe who they are and what they do, and above all explain why customers should leave these well established businesses in order to buy from you. Hopefully price will not be the only point of significance here. You should highlight all aspects of your marketing mix that will make you different and better.

7 Promotion. As a new business you need to explain how you will initially gain the attention of your potential customers and then how you will actually sell to them. Cover all the techniques mentioned in Chapter 10 that you will use such as advertising, public relations, direct mail, leaflets or brochures, promotions and personal selling whether face to face or over the telephone. The more detail you can include about exactly how you will get business the better. In order to complete the financial section of the plan you will have to have a very clear idea of the costs of your initial and ongoing promotional activities.

Location and premises

You may have already referred to this as one of the factors that will help you beat the competition. It is very important so more details need to be included. In particular you need to concentrate on explaining why the location and premises you have chosen are suitable for the kind of business you will pursue. You should cover:

1 Location. Describe the location and explain why you chose it.

2 Premises. Describe your premises, explain what makes them suitable for your operation, state whether you are buying or renting and if renting how long your lease will run. Point out also that you have covered all relevant regulations.

3 Costs. Run through all the costs, initial and ongoing, as described in Chapter 6.

4 Future needs. Will the premises be adequate to meet your future needs and if not what do you plan to do about it?

Financial projections: start-up costs

This section can go through all the items you need to start your business (as outlined in Chapter 11) taking care to explain why any seemingly questionable items are essential. Make your costings detailed but don't, at this stage, explain where the money is going to come from.

Financial projections: budget and cash flow forecast

This section covers your predicted financial performance and relates to Chapter 11. For both the budget and the cash flow forecast each bank may have its own forms. You should use the forms or at least follow the same format since this will make life easier for the bank manager who is accustomed to seeing the figures displayed in that way.

1 The budget. Complete a budget for your first year of trading. Make sure that you add footnotes beneath the budget to support the figures you have arrived at, especially for sales but also for estimated overheads. Some figures, such as those for advertising and promotion, you can link in with the relevant section of this business plan. You will need to make clear how you have arrived at your gross margin since it has such a crucial effect on your profitability and you should also point out that you are well aware of your breakeven level of sales, which you might split down into a monthly figure to act as a sales target.

2 The cash flow forecast. Although the budget will tell the bank manager if your business should be profitable, it does not tell him when this cash will pass through your business and therefore if you will require any additional short-term finance for working capital purposes. Fill in your cash flow forecast as explained in Chapter 11. Since you will have explained most points in your budget section few footnotes will be necessary unless the timing of a certain payment, for example the receipt of a grant, needs clarifying.

Financial requirements

It is now quite easy to explain your financial requirements and the type of loan you would like to meet them. You should divide this section of the plan into the following parts:

1 **Total borrowing requirement.** Your maximum borrowing requirement will be the highest figure generated in any month on your cash flow forecast form.

2 **Long-term borrowing requirement.** This will relate mainly to the items featured in your start-up costs which will have to be paid back over a number of years.

3 **Net loan required.** If you have a certain amount of capital of your own available to invest in the business you should make this clear now, deduct it from your long-term borrowing requirement and arrive at the net figure for the loan you require. You may specify a particular type of loan which you consider to be appropriate or you may leave this for discussion with the bank manager.

4 **Working capital requirements.** A proportion of your borrowings will be to cover short-term working capital requirements caused by a seasonal fall in sales or increase in stock. This sum will be the difference between the figures shown in 1 and 2 and will normally be covered by an overdraft facility with a limit of that amount or slightly more.

5 **Repayment proposals.** How will you repay the money? You should be able to cover the overdraft easily by showing on your cash flow forecast that the good months will, as time goes on, pay off the overdraft needed in the bad months.

Unless you have more cash of your own to inject at a later date (if necessary), the only way you will pay off the bank loan is by making a sufficiently high net profit to cover the repayments. Your financial projections will therefore show if you can afford to repay the size of loan you need to start your business, including the interest and service charges.

6 **Security.** Can you offer any security for the loan? If you are using the loan to purchase tangible assets can you offer the bank a charge over your business assets to cover at least part of the loan? Can you offer a personal guarantee to cover the outstanding amount? You will have to decide if you are prepared to offer any personal assets, such as your house, to secure all or part of the loan.

Presentation

As previously mentioned, presentation is vital. If the presentation of your business plan is anything other than immaculate, what does that suggest about the way you will present your product or service to customers? If the detail of the plan is not thorough and meticulously accurate, what does that suggest about the way you will manage your business? Everything communicates a message, so you must ensure that the right not the wrong impression is created. There now follows a brief explanation of several aspects of good presentation.

Packaging

Your business plan, like your products, must be well packaged. Of course, this means having it typed and it should also be bound with a quality report cover. The binding and cover can be done 'while you wait' at one of the high street print shops for no more than £5. Typing can be quite expensive, so it is worth trying to find a friend who will oblige.

Layout

There is a commonly accepted format for business reports which you should follow.

1 Title. You should start with a title page which will state simply in bold capitals, 'XYZ Ltd. Business Plan 1990-91'. At the foot of the page show the date on which the report was reproduced.

2 Overview. The next page will be a brief summary of the whole plan. This is not just a listing of topics but should emphasize the key points such as the purpose of the plan (for example, to raise finance), the company's background, product or service and objectives, and a very general summary of the financial projections, including predicted turnover, date when you expect to breakeven, and first year profit. You would end with a statement of your funding requirement. The whole thing should definitely take less than one page.

3 Contents. Next follows your contents page. Assuming you have kept to the format suggested in this chapter it should look like this:

CONTENTS

Overview

Contents

1. Background of the business
      1.1 Personal motives
      1.2 The nature of the business
      1.3 Preparations to date

2. Ownership and management
      2.1 Directors/Partners/Key managers (as relevant)
      2.2 Shareholders (if different from above)
      2.3 Employees

3. The product/service
3.1 Description of product(s)/service(s)
3.2 Manufacturing operations (if relevant)
3.3 Distinguishing features
3.4 Future development

4. Market analysis and marketing
4.1 Location of market
4.2 Market size
4.3 Market share (if relevant, may be covered in 4.2)
4.4 Market growth
4.5 Customers
4.6 Competitors
4.7 Sales and promotional activities

5. Location and premises
5.1 The location decision
5.2 Description of premises
5.3 Cost of premises
5.4 Future needs

6. Financial projections
6.1 Start-up costs
6.2 First year budget
6.3 Twelve month cash flow forecast

7. Financial requirements
7.1 Total borrowing requirement
7.2 Long-term borrowing requirement
7.3 Net loan required
7.4 Working capital requirements
7.5 Repayment proposals
7.6 Security

Appendices
1. Biographical details of key managers (if relevant)
2. Illustrations or technical drawings of the product
3. Market studies, articles from trade journals or other evidence to back up your statements in section 4
4. Promotional literature, if available
5. Plans or illustrations of premises if available and relevant
6. Names of professional advisers

4 Body of the report. This will proceed as outlined on the contents page with each new section starting on a new page. The appendices at the end will be used for any additional information which you think may be helpful but would be too detailed to be included in the body of the report. Make sure that the paragraphs are well spaced out for maximum clarity throughout.

All of this accomplished, you should have a very well presented business plan. More importantly you should have a well planned business. All that remains is to implement the plans!

Fig. 13.1 A good business plan is vital to ensure the success of your small business

Summary

1 Whether or not you require a loan, planning is a vital discipline for all business owners and managers to practise.

2 The first step is to write a business plan covering the first year of your new business.

3 The business plan will cover the people in the business, the thinking behind the business and the main areas of management and control of importance to the business.

4 Although the content is by far the most important aspect of the plan it could be let down by poor presentation. Great care should therefore be taken with format, layout and even superficial aspects such as binding to ensure that a good first impression is made.

Index